Reporting for Radio

Chuck Crouse

Radio-Televison News Directors Association

and

Bonus Books, Inc.

To Joe Zelle
For inspiration and support
early and often

96 95 94 93 92 5 4 3 2 1

Library of Congress Catalog Card Number: 92-73248

International Standard Book Number: 0-929387-88-0

Bonus Books, Inc.
160 East Illinois Street
Chicago, Illinois 60611

Printed in the United States of America

Contents

Preface

This book had its origin in a series of lectures for interns at WEEI-AM in Boston during the 1970's, and at several Boston-area colleges during the same era. I speculated that a manual specifically for radio news—as distinguished from "radio-TV news"—might be needed. I went so far as to draft a number of chapters, but set the project aside. Then, in 1985, a radio-news newsletter called *Earshot* ceased publication, and once again I felt that radio people needed some support. I approached Joe Tiernan, Editor of the *Communicator,* the monthly magazine published by the Radio-Television News Directors Association. He was very receptive, and the result was an approximately-monthly column, "Reporting for Radio", which continues to this day.

By 1991, a considerable amount of useful material had been published in that column, and discussions began about collecting that material between the covers of a book. This book, while intended primarily for college students and professionals in the first few years of their careers, may also be useful to radio news people with substantially more experience. I confess to having learned many of the techniques, or having acquired some of the insights here contained well past my tenth—oh, let's be honest—past my thirtieth anniversary in this business. Slow learners, take heart.

I undertook the process described above for one reason: I love radio, and I really believe in radio news. At several

pointsin the chapters that follow, the reader will find reasons why one might be well advised not to work in radio news. The reasons in favor of such a career must be discovered within oneself.

As any number of histories of the industry will relate, news was a major element in the creation of radio broadcasting. The 1920 U.S. presidential election figured prominently in the earliest broadcasts of two pioneer stations: WWJ, Detroit, and KDKA, Pittsburgh. As more stations came on the air, and as the first networks (AT&T and RCA in 1924, their merger into NBC in 1925, United Independent Broadcasters in 1927, and its transformation into CBS in 1928) were created, news was a major programming element.

In the early days, live broadcasts of special events overshadowed regularly-scheduled newscasts. Radio news milestones include the dedication of Baltimore's Francis Scott Key monument in 1923, ex-President Woodrow Wilson's 1923 appeal for U. S. entry into the League of Nations, the 17-day Democratic National Convention in 1924, and the inaugural address of President Calvin Coolidge and the Scopes "monkey trial", both in 1925. Neither network had a news department until 1932, when CBS began applying that term to what was in fact its publicity department.

Daily network newscasts arrived in 1929, in the voice of newspaper correspondent Floyd Gibbons who appeared on NBC for fifteen minutes each night, six nights a week. Adventurer Lowell Thomas began doing fifteen-minute newscasts on both NBC and CBS in 1930. For many years, fifteen-minute newscasts (often including considerable commentary) were the staple of the radio news day. A local station might schedule five minutes of news at 7 am, fifteen minutes at 8, five minutes at noon, fifteen minutes at 6 pm (perhaps followed by separate sports, business and commentary programs), and wrap up the day with a nightcap newscast at 11 pm. Hourly newscasts did not become common until World War Two, when listeners listened avidly for the latest word of various campaigns and battles.

Early newscasts were frequently written from newspapers or wire service dispatches. But as newspapers began to perceive radio as a competitor, they took action to impede use of print accounts on the air. After radio coverage of the election of Franklin Delano Roosevelt in 1932 (based largely on wire service reports) totally eclipsed newspaper coverage, newspaper publishers acted. They forced the Associated Press, which was newspaper-owned, to cease providing service to radio stations or networks. Under pressure, United Press and International News Service followed suit. CBS and NBC responded by forming their own news gathering operations. Within a year, the newspaper publishers offered a compromise. A bureau was established, which re-wrote wire copy and supplied two daily five-minute newscast scripts. Subscribing broadcasters were required to wait until 9:30 am and 9:00 pm (after the hours of highest readership of morning and afternoon papers) to air the scripts. This, too, did not last. A competing wire service, Transradio Press, was established, as were regional news services for radio stations. By 1936, UP had a radio wire of its own, with no restrictions.

If the hourly newscast was born during World War Two, it reached adolescence during the years after the war. Hundreds of new stations went on the air at that time, many of them not affiliated with networks. The new independents filled much of their air time with records played by disc jockeys, a comparatively new phenomenon. A five-minute newscast at the top of each hour satisfied FCC requirements for non-entertainment programming and offered a competitive alternative to the widely separated news blocks scheduled by the network stations.

With the coming of Top 40 radio (analagous to today's Contemporary Hit Radio format) in the mid-1950's, hourly newscasts fluorished. Early Top 40 programmers believed that a fast-moving newscast, short on issues but long on police and fire news, complemented the rapid-fire deejay shows. As traditional radio network programming died out under competition from television, the four major networks (Mutual was created in

1934, and ABC was split off from NBC in 1943) added hourly newscasts to their schedules. Ironically, it was the Top 40 stations and their successors who then led the move to drop hourly newscasts. As competition among music-intensive stations increased, programmers came to see news as a tune-out factor. Newscasts were dropped after 6 pm, when the listening audience was more heavily composed of teenagers. Stations seeking to build their daytime audiences by catering to people at work discontinued midday newscasts. After the FCC ended most of its regulation of programming in the early 1980's, many music-intensive stations (chiefly on the FM band) dropped all newscasts after 9 am.

As music stations began to steer away from news, other stations (chiefly AM) went to the other extreme. In 1960, KFAX (AM) in San Francisco was the first station in the U.S. to experiment with an all-news format. Westinghouse introduced its "all news, all the time" format on New York's WINS (AM) in 1965. CBS jumped on the bandwagon with WCBS-AM in 1967. All-news stations have blossomed (and sometimes withered) in most major markets over the years.

As a field of endeavor, radio news has become larger and more professional. Until the mid-1950's, there were very few reporters, except at the network level. A small station might employ a single newscaster, and assign staff announcers (disc jockeys) to rip news from the wire at other hours. Larger stations might boast morning and afternoon newscasters, and possibly even an evening newscaster. Only the largest employed a "street reporter", whose job was to travel around the city, covering breaking news in voice reports by telephone or two-way radio. News people typically were disc jockeys who made the transition or ex-newspaper and wire service reporters. Many had no college training.

Through the 1960's, this picture changed drastically. Technology allowed more reporting from the field. News-intensive stations in larger markets acquired staffs of ten or more people. Major all-news stations had 25 news staffers or more. And employers came to value college education in candidates for news positions. Broadcast communications emerged from the shadow of speech or theater departments at larger universities, or became separate divisions within schools of journalism.

Technological change has fostered much of this growth. Early live broadcasts required a small truck filled with bulky tube-type equipment. A live broadcast from the scene required at least one technician to operate the gear. As late as the early 1960's the standard "portable" tape recorder weighed 26 pounds, and had to be plugged into a wall outlet. A few miniature battery-operated recorders existed, but were costly or unreliable. The introduction of the cassette recorder by Dutch-owned North American Phillips (Norelco) in 1966 sparked a revolution. Suddenly, high-quality recording of events outside the station was easy and cheap. Reporting from the field became commonplace. The introduction of lightweight cellular telephones in the late 1980's gave reporters a freedom that broadcasters of a generation earlier could only have dreamed.

For all of the programming and technological progress outlined in the preceding paragraphs, radio news today seems to be in a period of transition. The economics of radio has imposed severe limits on staffing. Deregulation by the FCC has encouraged music stations to eliminate news from most parts of the program day. Young broadcasters are entering the field better prepared than ever, but are finding less reason to be sanguine about prospects of a career in radio. Many choose television instead. Despite all of this, audience surveys consistently show that upwards of 97 percent of all adults listen to radio in a given week, and that a large percentage of them get first word of breaking stories from the radio. Time will tell whether radio will give up its role as a major provider of news coverage, or find a new footing on which to rebuild its strength.

Acknowledgments

Because of the broad scope of this book, every co-worker and competitor I've ever been exposed to has had a part in it, because they've contributed to my understanding of radio news. The following people—some deceased, some listed by air name—either are the source of specific points I include or were directly involved in the preparation of the *Communicator* column or of this book. I am grateful to all for their many forms of assistance over the years. Any errors of fact or interpretation are, of course, my own.

Robert Ames, Don Amstutz, Rolfe Auerbach, Larry Barr, Pat Beaudry, Larry Blanke, Randy Brock, Steve Brown, Andrea Carniero, Pat Carroll, Ed Clancy, Tracy Cole, Bob Conrad, Irene Cornell, Ken Courtright, Susan Darwin, Don Davis, Len Davis, Harry Dennis, Walt Dibble, Lynn Distler, Dick Drury, Dick Ertmann, Peter Finch, Steve Flanders, Bernard Gershon, Rick Gevers, Daryl Gould and Gordon Govier.

Also Jack Harper, Gene Hartigan, Fred Honsberger, Carla Johnston, Jon Kent, David Levin, Dick Levitan, Jim Londot, Jim Long, Mike Ludlum, Bill Lynch, Chris Lyons, Jim Martin, John Masters, Owen May, Willis McCaleb, Phil

McLean, Kevin McNicholas, Bob Michaels, Gerri Miller, Mel Miller, Pete Mobilia, Will Murphy, Diane Novak, Evelyn Nowell, Bob Oakes, Ed Perry, Liz Randolph, Carl Reese, John Rodman and Pat Romano.

Also Peter Salinger, Harry Savas, Steve Sbraccia, Lee Schell, Louise Schiavone, Bob Segal, Linda Sherman, Ira Sills, Phil Sirkin, Phil Smith, Carl Stevens, Merrie Street, Diane Sutter, Joe Tierney, Neil Ungerleider, Walt Wheeler, Holly Wolfe, Les Woodruff, Joe Zelle and George Zucker.

CHAPTER 1

The Newscast

One may ask why a book on reporting begins with a chapter on newscasts. The answer, implicit in the thumbnail historical sketch in the Preface, is that the newscast is the most fundamental form of radio reporting. The newscaster says to the listener, in effect, "Here's what's going on that I think you'll find important and interesting." That statement (usually left unspoken) amounts to a promise. The newscaster has two ways to keep the promise: 1) story selection and 2) writing.

Story Selection

One of the oldest and most thoroughly debated questions in journalism is "What is news?" Among the working definitions are "what touches people", "what interests people", and "what people need to know to function in a self-governing society." More than one authority has proposed the "how-about-that" criterion. If a story would cause a listener, sitting at the breakfast table or in a car, to say to the person with him or her, "How about that!", it's news.

No single criterion governs exclusively. Your own judgement, involving an understanding of the needs and interests of the people in your community and of the target audience your station seeks, will play a major role. Political news scores well on a "need-to-know" scale, but tends not to interest listeners of a youth-oriented rock music station. That station's newscaster would have to handle political stories with great care to avoid tune-outs. Kickers and celebrity stories taken one at a time may interest people, but a newscast composed entirely of such stories would strike many listeners as shallow.

Other factors enter into story selection. Plainly, if your station carries hourly newscasts from a network, your own newscasts are likely to be predominently, if not wholly, local and state news. "Easy listening" stations sometimes choose to downplay police news as conflicting with the goal of helping the listener relax. Two stations in a sizeable city surrounded by farming areas may have different policies on farm news, because the more powerful station will reach farther into rural areas than the lower-power station. A small-town station may use a story about an attempted break-in at a dry cleaner, while a big-city station may not report burglaries at all, unless there is something really remarkable, such as a million-dollar art heist.

In general, the newest story is likely to lead, but a fairly trivial "new" story may run following a continuing story of considerable importance. Thus, a meeting being held in hopes of ending your community's teachers' strike may lead for hours, even though newer stories such as routine traffic accidents or passage of a secondary bill in the legislature are available.

Lineups are often based on whether stories are local, state, national or international in origin. Years ago, it was common to lead with national and international news, then move on to local and state stories. A shift in the British cabinet would overshadow a double-fatal at the main intersection of the station's city of license. Stations emphasizing local identity may make story selections that are just as lopsided. There is no single "correct" lineup of stories in a given day's flow of news, but there are also many that are inappropriate. Your audience will tend to accept your judgements at face value, unless your choice is egregiously inappropriate.

In general, there should be a flow of stories within a newscast. If you lead with a local crime story, it may be best to group it with other local police stories before moving on to government, economics or feature material. A Washington lead may best flow to any other Washington stories you want to include, before moving on. But there's no rule that a newscast must always lead with crime, or with politics or any other category. Neither must a newscast cover all national stories before going local, or vice versa. Here's an example of a balanced newscast lineup which uses some story grouping:

Mideast peace talks—new development	:15
Mideast violence—audio service wrap	:45
Local environmental problem—actuality	:30
Local city council hearing preview	:20
State legislative story	:20
Crime in distant county of state—voicer	:35
Space shuttle launch plans	:15
Entertainment kicker	:15
	3:15

Now let's knock that lineup into a cocked hat. Suppose that, five minutes before air time, your police scanner brings word of a serious auto accident near your town. You have time to call for confirmation of the basics and to type up a two-sentence story. Presumably, that story would lead. What changes need to be made to the newscast? You'll need to remove one story to avoid running long. If you are talking to a young audience, you may choose to drop the legislative story. But the space shuttle story may be expendable if there's nothing really remarkable about the mission, or the launch is still a day or so away.

To continue with hypothetical last-minute developments, suppose the story were the discovery of a body nearby. You would probably lead . . . and bring up the distant-county voicer to run second, before going to the Mideast. But be careful: the body may not necessarily be that of someone who died of foul play.

Now suppose the last-minute story is a fairly serious earthquake in South America. Until details are known, you may choose not to lead with it, but to run it in place of the space shuttle story. However, if your city has a large Hispanic population, you might choose to place it higher in the 'cast.

In other words, each story added to a newscast lineup changes the entire mix. For this reason, it's wise to keep stories fanned out, from writing through broadcast, so that you always have an instant view of the newscast as a whole.

Special Cases

The tyranny of the clock often forces difficult choices. Suppose you have lined up most of a newscast with stories you feel *must* go in, and have thirty seconds left. There remain two good local stories. One is about the non-fatal shooting, a few hours ago, of a local man. The second is about the opening, tomorrow morning, of a long-awaited local highway bridge which will be traversed by thousands of cars each day. What to do?

You may be inclined to favor the shooting story, because it's a serious crime, local and recent. You may lean toward the bridge opening, because it will touch the lives of so many motorists. (In deciding, remember that the jock is very cantankerous, and gets upset when a newscast runs long.)

All right, the "Jeopardy" music ends, and the correct answer is . . . use both stories! Remember, you had thirty seconds to fill. So tell the shooting story in twenty seconds, and kiss off the bridge opening in two short sentences running ten seconds.

Another seeming "either-or" choice is resolved in the following example: armed terrorists have been holding a building in a major city in the United States for many hours, as police SWAT teams and helicopters surround the scene. Meanwhile, a fire has just broken out at a junkyard in your city, sending a column of dark smoke billowing high into the sky. Afternoon drive is beginning, and most of your listeners are in cars, wondering about the building takeover, *and* looking at that unexplained pall of smoke.

The solution, as outlined by Walt Dibble, a veteran Connecticut radio news director, is the following:

"Fire in an Ourtown junkyard is sending a huge cloud of smoke high into the sky. Details in a moment, but first, here's the latest on that terrorist building takeover in Faraway City."

Writing the Newscast

As already noted, a newscast is an assemblage of separate stories. So we'll begin by analyzing the process of writing a news story. I find it helpful to visualize the factoids—information elements such as name, time, location—as little blobs of matter on a table . . . beads to be strung, perhaps. (But certainly not jigsaw puzzle pieces, because there is only one way to put a jigsaw puzzle together.) We remove the factoids from the table and group them into sentences, bearing in mind that the listener can assimilate only such much information at a time. Consider the following one-sentence story:

> Two Nextville men, 32-year old Joseph Doe of 145 Zilch Street, and 29-year old Marvin Moe of 67 Foonman Terrace, were arrested by Ourtown police just before four this morning, allegedly emerging from Bauble's Jewelers at Third and Main with watches and jewelry valued at more than fifteen thousand dollars, and will be arraigned later this morning before Municipal Judge Hosmer Wump on charges of second degree burglary, the penalty for conviction of which is three to five years in prison.

The story as written gets all relevant factoids off the table, but leaves the listener hopelessly behind, well before the halfway point. The only thing the sample one-sentence story has going for it is that it does arrange the factoids in approximately the order needed for listener comprehension. To begin the story with the judge's name, the time of the arrest or the penalty upon conviction would produce a story that was even more clumsy and unlikely to hold the listener's attention. Now let's un-string the beads and try again. To help understand the function of each sentence, we will label them.

Two Nextville men are under arrest this morning for a pre-dawn burglary at an Ourtown jewelry story.	**Lead Sentence.** Essential factoids are included, but we don't name suspects or store.
Ourtown police say they nabbed 32-year old Joseph Doe of 145 Zilch Street and 29-year old Marvin Moe of 67 Foonman Terrace, just before four am.	**Development Sentence.** Contains attribution, time and names of suspects. Ages and street numbers are optional, helpful if there may be more than one person with this name in your city.
The two were allegedly emerging from Bauble's Jewelers at Third and Main carrying watches and jewelry worth more than fifteen thousand dollars.	**Development sentence.** Continues the narrative.
The suspects are charged with second degree burglary, and will be arraigned this morning before Municipal Judge Hosmer Wump.	**Wrapup sentence.** Contains the remaining relevant factoids and looks forward to next probable event. Penalty is omitted: who cares?

A shorter story might omit the suspects' ages and street numbers, as well as the judge's name. In small markets, on the other hand, it is often the practice to include the names of arresting officers.

A disciplined and analytical writer, aware of the Lead-Development-Wrapup sequence, can write many of the stories that come along in three sentences, keeping sentence length under control and enhancing listener comprehension. To illustrate further condensation, we'll write the burglary story again, but in just two sentences:

Two Nextville men face arraignment this morning, on charges of burglarizing Bauble's Jewelry in Ourtown.	We move the next-step element and store name into the Lead Sentence.
Police say Joseph Doe of Zilch Street and Marvin Moe of Foonman Terrace were carrying more than fifteen thousand dollars worth of loot when they were nabbed just before four am.	Development sentence contains attribution, names, value of loot and time of arrest. We omit ages, street numbers and description of loot. (If they were stealing lawnmowers from the jewelry store, it might be a different matter.)

The second sentence is a bit long, but manageable if you take a breath just after the word "loot." The story leaves unanswered the question "How were they arrested?" (As they were emerging from the store), but we're trying to keep this version short. Something has to go.

I once analyzed a newscast aired by a national radio network, and discovered that every story was two sentences long. At about the same time, I observed that a major wire service wrote most of the stories in its five-minute summaries in three sentences.

Must all stories in a newscast be the same length? Not at all. The sample story lineup earlier in this chapter shows typical variations in length. An extreme case occurred the day after David Berkowitz was arrested for the "Son of Sam" murders in New York City. WOR-AM broadcast a fifteen-minute newscast at noon which had thirteen minutes on Son of Sam, and two other stories, each about ten seconds in length.

While the broadcaster is well advised to stick to a straight, complete-sentence style of writing in most cases, it is instructive to observe how some skilled practitioners of the craft depart from the norm. Perhaps the best example is Paul Harvey, whose highly personalized broadcasts on ABC set the outer limits of writing style. Some years ago, when heart transplants were still extremely rare and each one was covered in detail, Harvey demonstrated his understanding of the average listener's close attention to one lingering case. His story was: "Mike Kasperak: still critical. Six days now." So closely was the case followed that Harvey felt no need to say who Mike Kasperak was. Paul Harvey, of course, has a franchise to do highly stylized stories, and most other broadcasters do not. Having written a hundred thousand news stories or so for practice helps, if one plans to go out on that particular limb.

It is important to keep delivery in mind while writing a newscast. The copy will be spoken aloud, and will reach the listener through his or her ears, not eyes. Writing which works in print may not communicate well aurally. Consider these factors:

- Oral vs. written style. Words, phrases or syntax which are quite acceptable on the printed page may strike the ear as stilted. "Clandestine" may better be changed to "secret", "prowess" to "skill." "The weapon with which he took Smith's life" becomes "the gun he used to kill Smith." "And/or" and "etcetera" are best left to committee chairmen reading reports.

- Homophones. Avoid "halve": it sounds like "have"; "wholly" like "holy" and "cache" like "cash."
- Double negatives. "The court struck down a law banning kite flying" might better be written, "The court in effect ruled that kite flying is legal." "Snow is not uncommon at this time of year" is not without fault.
- Breath control. Read copy aloud as you write it, to spot writing that leaves the newscaster no place to take a breath. Short sentences eliminate the problem.
- Cadence. We are not writing nineteenth-century orations. Nor are we writing poetry. But there are rhythms which sound graceful, and those which sound choppy or abrupt.

Yes, we often write in a hurry. But speaking the words in your head, then reading the copy aloud, will eliminate most pitfalls that will await you (or someone else) in the studio.

Writing can be done in many different styles, and the broadcaster, being a generalist, should be able to use several. A story about preparations for a prominent person's funeral should not have the same tone or texture as one about the circus coming to town. A story about a trial or lawsuit requires much greater care than one about a frisbee contest. I make no case for pompous or silly writing, only for writing whose tone matches the topic.

The words on the paper are only part of the story you write. Punctuation sends distinct messages as to how the words are to be read. Each period, comma, semi-colon, colon or dash has a specific meaning. Some broadcast writers like to throw out all conventional punctuation and use ellipsis marks (. . .) separating phrases. Some writers go even farther, typing in all capitals, as old-fashioned teletype machines (which had no lower-case letters) did. This sends the newscaster into the studio with one hand tied behind his or her back, because the information contained in the use of capitals in upper-and-lower-case typing and in punctuation marks, is absent. A claim that adopting the more literate practices "just slows me down" only implies that the speaker hasn't taken time to learn them. Once learned, they take no longer than the more clumsy practices. The task at hand is to sound good. Use all the tools at your disposal.

This chapter assumes that a newscast is assembled from stories written one per sheet of paper, not written integrally on a single sheet of paper (or two or three, if needed). Granted, the time it takes to crank separate sheets of paper into the typewriter does add up (more so if a word processor is used). But the integral newscast cannot be revised at the last minute. The stories are in a fixed order. Changing that order requires drawing arrows and brackets, and invites losing one's place.

Further, writing discrete stories allows one story to be recycled at one hour, and another to be re-used at a different hour. An integral newscast, if recycled, is more easily identified as a repeat than is a mixture of separate stories drawn from several earlier newscasts. There is also a temptation, when writing an integral newscast, to insert unnecessary transitional phrases, like "Here at home . . .", or "In political news . . ."

Style, Not Fashion

Some newcomers to broadcasting get the idea that, because they work in an oral medium, good writing is not important. They forget that most of what is said on the air is in fact read. And bad writing, when read aloud, doesn't sound any better.

Contemporary observers sometimes claim that we are becoming a post-literate society. What that means is that we may not look down on illiteracy as much as we once did. But bad use of our common language is still bad English, and it shows.

Good grammar is still essential to communicating clearly on the air. Yes, broadcasters no longer sound as formal as they once did. But "conversational" is not a synonym for "slovenly."

For example, some broadcasters are in the habit of omitting forms of "to be" (be, am, is, are, was, were) when writing a story. This practice produces such atrocities as "Police holding a robbery suspect this morning." The listener, thinking he or she has heard the front half of a sentence, waits for the rest of it (". . . say they have recovered three stolen TV sets.") But the wait is in vain, as the newscaster goes on to another sentence. The broadcaster who defends this practice as in some way "conversational" need only ask himself whether he has ever heard a non-broadcaster talk this way. He has not. Nor has he heard other broadcasters talk that way in off-air conversation.

While good grammar and accuracy should be the first tests applied to writing for broadcast, graceful use of the language is of nearly equal importance. Your words should not clump across the stage like a ballerina in combat boots. If your news story sounds like a cop on the witness stand, or like a bureaucrat at a public hearing, you have strayed. The murder victim did not "expire after sustaining a gunshot wound to the upper left temple"; he "died after being shot in the head." The legislative committee will not "convene for the purpose of ascertaining the effectiveness of the new program's implementation"; it will "meet to see how well the new program is working."

Clear away the buzzwords, the cliches and the trendy non-grammar. Use verbs. Save fragments for those times when they actually help the story. Make run-ons and most parentheticals into separate sentences. Avoid "cutesy" leads. If you do all of these things, you will probably be left with clear, concise, easy-to-understand (not to mention easy to read) copy. And *that* is always in style, no matter what the fad of the moment may be.

For Those Who Just Tuned In

Imagine that you go to the window, and a freight train is passing on the track outside. You don't know whether the first car you see is the third or seventeenth, whether the car before it was a box car or a tank car, and, as you turn away, whether there remain two cars in the train or thirty. So it is with radio, an entirely linear medium. And we should be aware of that fact as we broadcast the news. There is always someone who just tuned in and did not hear what came before.

Let's take an obvious example. You write a story about a disaster in a distant city. The location appears in the lead. Then you give details of the casualties and damage. The longer the story is, the greater the likelihood that listeners have tuned in after the location was given and are anxious to know whether someone they know is affected. It's worth taking time to re-state the location late in the last sentence of the story.

Those who do analyses of ratings books are sometimes surprised by the brevity of the average listener's tune-in. Few listen hour after hour. More typical are tune-ins of from fifteen to forty-five minutes. If you have a story with strong interest, it's a mistake to omit it, saying, "Oh, I ran that one last newscast." Use a different write-up, perhaps a different actuality, for those who did hear the preceding newscast. But don't short-change those who tuned in during the intervening half-hour or hour.

This leads to a philosophical aside: is it good practice to begin, "Here's the latest on that water main break . . .", when the last on-air mention was thirty or sixty minutes earlier? Most listeners didn't hear the earlier mention. Does the wording in question make the listener feel left out, included, or motivated to listen more often? Presumably, news writers who use such a lead believe that it gives the same information as would be included in a more traditional lead, but with the bonus of a greater sense of urgency.

(A related question is whether it's a good idea to introduce your traffic reporter, last heard twenty minutes earlier, with, "Let's find out about that big backup on Route 24 . . ." I suspect the listener who has just tuned in feels a sudden anxiety surge: WHAT big backup on Route 24? It may depend on how hard you want to hit your listener's hot button. Less jarring might be, "Some problems on Route 24 this afternoon. Here's Kim with traffic.")

There is also something comforting about the realization that listeners are continually tuning in. Those listeners give you a fresh start, if you're having a bad day. Broadcasters often find that one flub leads to another, even in short newscasts. In all-news anchoring, a few blunders—and the embarassment one feels at having committed them—can cause a real downward spiral. At such a time, it is helpful to tell yourself that there's always a listener who has just tuned in, and hasn't heard any mistakes yet. With this listener, the slate is clean. Focus on that listener, and you can usually get back on track.

Three Newsroom "Musts"

1. Information received over the police/fire scanner cannot be used directly on the air. You *must* call the agency involved and confirm each and every fact contained in the transmission.

2. Before recording a telephone interview, you *must* obtain the interviewee's permission, no matter how often you interview the individual, even if he or she called seeking to be interviewed. "May I have your permission to record your voice for broadcast?" covers all the bases.

3. If you run a story in which an individual is personally attacked, you *must* seek out that individual and offer him or her an opportunity to respond.

C H A P T E R 2

Basic Reporting

Before we can broadcast the news, we must find some. The simplest expedient is taking it off the wire; the second-simplest, taking it out of the newspaper. More difficult but (most will agree) more satisfying, and of greater value to the listening public, is rounding up stories on our own.

Just Who Is a Reporter, Anyway?

Some time back, a colleague working at a radio station in New England wanted a piece for a newscast on an event which had happened the night before in a large midwestern city. He telephoned a station in that city and asked for a feed. "Oh," came the reply, "we don't go out and TAPE stuff." And that, in a backhanded way, is what a reporter is all about.

There are very few fulltime radio street reporters: perhaps a couple of hundred in the entire country, most at all-news stations or very large stations in top markets. Much more common is the radio newsperson who spends part of the day doing newscasts, and part of it reporting. Particularly in smaller markets, the News Director (often the only newsperson on the staff) takes about an hour during the mid-morning to "make the rounds." A whirlwind tour of the police and fire stations, the Mayor's office, the Sheriff, County Commissioners and perhaps the Chamber of Commerce (my list at WLKR, Norwalk, Ohio) isn't quite the same as covering a five-day-a-week beat at City Hall or the State House, or prowling the streets in a news cruiser for an entire shift. But all are radio news reporting, and the similarities in purpose and technique are more important than the differences.

The reporter exists to gather news directly, to be the eyes and ears of the station and of its listeners. A lot of news can be covered from the desk, mostly by telephone, but that often amounts to second-hand coverage. Since news happens outside the station, it takes someone in the field to cover it first-hand: to catch the sounds, the feel and the nuances of what transpires. Councilman Smith can tell you over the phone that he has a great new proposal. But it takes a reporter at the meeting to observe that Smith's fellow members of City Council all look bored and start going through their mail when he speaks, indicating that the proposal stands little chance of becoming reality. And the reporter in the field can tell you long before the desk sergeant can, whether the workers trapped in the cave-in were still alive when they were placed in the ambulance.

The radio reporter—the fulltime one, anyway—is something of a luxury, when measured by one yardstick. He or she generates perhaps eight or ten minutes a day of programming for the station, while the in-studio newscaster is good for five or ten minutes an hour, and the disc jockey can keep the carrier modulated for hours at a time. There must be something to justify that luxury. Actually, there are several things: immediacy, accuracy and credibility chief among them.

It must be acknowledged that radio news reporting is not as glamorous as it may appear. (Hundreds of heads are nodding in agreement . . .) Yes, the reporter gets to go places and meet people that "ordinary" people don't. But the job also involves a lot more hunting for parking spaces, rushing back to make the next 'cast, cajoling uncooperative officials, sitting through long meetings, getting rained on, and just plain waiting than the stories they produce even hint at. The radio reporter is more a guerilla moving self-contained and resourceful through the world than a roving celebrity. (If your mother wants to think otherwise, let her.)

Beyond actually gathering news, the radio reporter serves several important purposes. First, he or she is a building block of the newscast. Through voice reports, whether live or fed on tape, the reporter provides a change of voice from the anchor, seizing the listener's attention. By having been present at the scene, he or she provides an element of believability that even the finest newscaster has a hard time achieving in the studio. And since the reporter's piece is likely to be longer and more detailed than the anchor's reader, the piece gives the listener a fuller and more informative account.

As much as anyone on the staff, and more than most, the reporter represents the station to the "real world" beyond the studio doors. He or she is visible evidence of the station's news effort. The manager and sales force are out among the business community, providing important human contact. The reporter provides the same contact, to a broader cross-section of the community.

Finally, through his or her presence, the reporter establishes and maintains news sources. Once established, he or she can draw upon those sources in the future for additional stories or bits of information. Those names and phone numbers (well, most of them—some may be confidential) wind up in the newsroom Rolodex, helping others on the staff. And if the reporter is really good with people, the rapport that is established will lead many of them to step forward with followups or even entirely new stories, calling the station or at least mailing in news releases.

If the foregoing has the heads of one- and two-person news departments shrugging and saying, "Yeah, I sure wish we could afford a reporter!", then some encouragement is in order. Professor Vernon Stone's annual staff surveys, published in the RTNDA *Communicator,* tell us that the majority of radio news departments consist of three or fewer people. That's just enough to cover airshifts, right? Wrong. At some point during the day, most newspeople have time to get out, and do. It may be the midmorning rounds described earlier, it may be a couple of hours at the beginning of the afternoon anchor's shift, or it may be a couple of hours after the morning anchor gets off the air. But any time you leave the station, using your skills to search out new stories or angles on existing stories, looking for sound that helps tell the story, you're a reporter and you have plenty of company, in large markets and small.

The Reporter's Conceit

What? Reporters conceited? Why, we're all just level-headed down-to-earth folks, right? In truth, even those of us who are models of humility do embody a pretty substantial conceit—one so pervasive that we seldom notice it.

Let us join the typical radio newsperson as he or she leaves for work, cassette recorder slung over one shoulder. Said reporter has been trained in journalism, or broadcasting, or maybe English or political science. If typical, he or she is reasonably interested in the world, took a single course in economics in college, and reads *Newsweek* (but not *Foreign Affairs*) and perhaps *Prevention* (but not the AMA Journal).

Thus prepared, what does our "typical" radio reporter cover, either in person or by telephone? Well, the local medical school has an announcement of a development in AIDS research, the Appeals Court has overturned a lower court's ruling that the city can tax real estate transfers, and a large local company calls in reporters to announce a corporate restructuring following three consecutive "down" quarters. Since the station is fresh out of physicians, constitutional lawyers or MBA's on its news staff, we know who gets sent.

And there you have the Reporter's Conceit: we are generalists, called upon of necessity to cover stories which require specialized knowledge, for an audience which includes individuals who know more about those topics than we do. And we can gloss over only so much, or make only so many mistakes, before those listeners who catch us at it stop forgiving us.

Faced with this challenge, how does our radio reporter respond? Intimidated by the complexity of it all, he or she may just keep silent and hope there's enough in the handout material, or judge's opinion, to get by on. And sometimes there is. Fearful of sounding stupid, our scribe may refrain from asking a "dumb" (elementary) question, unaware that all the other reporters in the room are doing the same thing. Or our reporter may screw up the courage to say out loud, "Excuse me, but I don't know much about this. Could you give us some background?"

If our imaginary reporter chooses the latter option, several interesting things will happen. First, the other reporters in the room will silently thank him or her for having the nerve to ask. Second, the official with the answers will probably set aside the jargon and give a pretty good explanation, not having realized before that he or she was leaving the reporters behind. And third, a more accurate, informative story will be written. Admitting one's ignorance is uncomfortable and seems risky at the time, but pays long-term dividends.

Recognizing that we don't know it all is important in more circumstances than those cited above. That attention to factual detail—names, dates, titles and numbers—sets the "pro" apart from the beginner. Approximations and guesses are asking for trouble. Better to sound a fool to Mr. Big's secretary by calling back to ask for his first name, than to sound a fool to the hundreds or thousands who know that it's George, not John. ("Well, I thought I remembered somebody saying it was John.") And when you call him Chairman of the Park Board, when he's really Executive Secretary of the Public Works Commission, few will buy an excuse like, "Well, it's not important. We write conversationally here."

In Search of the Story

Let's start with the assumption that if a jetliner crashes on the outskirts of town, it's a news story. And if a cop hands out a ticket for overtime parking at a meter, it probably isn't. (How about if it's Madonna's car?) We earn our keep, among other ways, by being able to spot where, between those extremes, to draw the news/not-news line. Some examples:

Many years ago, at a small station in Norwalk, Ohio, I ran a story one Saturday afternoon about an auto accident at the town's main intersection. There were no injuries, no property damage and no citation. My reasoning was that it was the only current happening, and a good many people saw the incident because of its central location. Needless to say, it wasn't a very *long* story.

While working for WCBS-AM, I observed that most of the homicides that came over the police wire did not end up on the air. The reasoning there was that so many people die violently in such a big metropolitan area, a homicide had to have something that made it unique if it was to qualify as news.

A reporter named Donald E. Amstutz worked for a station in Van Wert, Ohio. In that small town, traffic arrests were considered news. One day, as he was driving downtown to make his rounds, he ran a red light and was pulled over by a police officer. That noon, Don Amstutz had as an item on his newscast the arrest of one "D. E. Amstutz" for a red light violation. (No one made the connection.)

Having grown up in the Philadelphia and Cleveland areas, I took awhile to get used to small-town news values. When the boss told me about a new gas station being planned, I yawned. He then explained that in a town of 13,000, an investment of a hundred thousand dollars in a business which would provide five new jobs was significant. He was right.

It was that same boss who explained, in its simplest terms, the law of enterprise reporting: If you're walking down the street and you see some men digging a hole, stop and ask, "Hey, whatcha digging the hole for?"

A somewhat more elaborate example of looking closely at the obvious occurred one afternoon in a medium-sized city, when a messenger delivered a news release from one of the city's largest financial businesses. The headline had to do with a program being set up to develop management potential in executives. "Corporate ego," yawned the newscaster who received the release. "Sending this dreck by messenger." But the newscaster kept reading, and halfway down the second page, the release said the development program was being undertaken in the context of the resignation that day of the company's President and Chief Executive Officer. In other words, they had just fired their president, and were taking steps to make sure that they didn't get any more turkeys in high places. That station led with it. No other broadcast outlet used the story. The morning newspaper reached the same conclusion the radio guy did. *Then* the other radio stations picked it up.

Compare the previous with this concluding (and possibly apocryphal) anecdote: The reporter was sent to cover a meeting of City Council. He returned a while later, and went about some other news duties. The News Director asked about the City Council story. The reporter replied, "They didn't have a meeting."

"Why?", asked the ND.

"Oh, they couldn't use the Council Chamber."

"They couldn't?"

"No. The building was on fire."

Objectivity versus Fairness

Supposedly, a reporter is or tries to be totally objective as he or she covers stories. In reality, that's not possible, since no two reporters look at an event or issue through the same eyes. They have different backgrounds, experiences and values. With the best of intentions, two reporters will tell a story differently. That, after all, is the foundation on which the American tradition of diversity of news outlets is built.

Since *objectivity* is an ideal best left to computers, what many reporters strive for instead is *fairness*. It's more easily achieved, but harder to define. A substantial portion of the populace defines fair as "that which is favorable to me." It is no such thing. Simply (and circularly) put, it is "what you've got coming." If public figure X deserves a pat on the back, a fair news account should allow the listener to reach that conclusion. If public figure Y deserves a kick in the pants, that too, should be evident. Granted the public figure and the reporter may differ on whether a pat or a kick is appropriate, and that's where things get sticky.

People unused to operating in that fuzzy area between objectivity and fairness may find it difficult at first to separate personal reaction from a fair account. If a neophyte reporter hears a speaker utter what to him or her is total balderdash, the inclination may be to find the most direct way possible to tell the public that the speaker is a menace to the Republic. With a bit more experience, the reporter may swing to the opposite extreme, and show how "objective" he or she is by reporting precisely what was said and no more. I submit that neither approach is a good thing, but that the second at least gives the listener some unfiltered facts from which to draw a conclusion.

Preferable, but harder to achieve, is the story which gives the listener a clear picture of what happened, with just enough analysis to let the listener know where a grain of salt may be helpful. Seasoned reporters will differ on just when and by how much a straight account should be augmented by analysis. Some difficult questions are involved: Where is the balance between the obligation to let the public figure communicate his positions and policies to the people, and the obligation to the audience to let them know when the public figure may be lying through his or her teeth or patently acting without sincerity? What obligation have you to the listener to make it clear that the public figure was manipulating the press or grandstanding?

Part of the answer is that most people aren't as dumb as is often thought, and the public figure's own words may damn him. Careful selection of quotes or sound bites may give the listeners the clues they need. However, no "pro" comes away from every speech or news conference *looking* for the cut that makes the newsmaker sound most like a fool.

Another part of the answer is that relevant facts may be inserted into a story, when "Mayor Smith spoke the following words . . ." fails to tell the whole truth. You may find yourself writing "Speaking with crumbs all over his mouth, Mayor Smith told reporters he knew of no cookie jars in City Hall." If the promised "major proposal" turns out to be a replay of something already put forth, the reporter can take note of the fact, perhaps including date and place of the previous occcasion. If the speaker fills his or her remarks with phrases such as ". . . and your tremendous support tonight shows that the public is behind my plan . . .", you may be able to recall that this rally drew fewer than half as many people as attended a rally held by the opposition a few days earlier. But be careful: the opposition may just be better at drumming up a crowd.

Best of all is simply to afford those with differing points of view an opportunity to be heard. Let Councilwoman Zilch point out that the Mayor is taking credit for something the state was already doing of its own accord. That, after all, is what "public debate" is. And it spares you the difficult task of waving the red flags.

On the other hand, you may cover an event or speaker which leaves you filled with admiration. Again, caution is necessary. The temptation may be strong to give the story an especially positive tone. Reporters are no more cheerleaders than they are prosecutors.

In the end, how a reporter brings to the listener's attention the facts that aren't obvious in a straight account can say as much about the reporter as it does about the public figure.

The Hometown Pitfall

The reporter who finds himself working in the area in which he grew up faces a special pitfall. He (or she) may find himself covering people he went to school with. He must be prepared to run into such people in circumstances which may show those old friends and acquaintances in an unfavorable light. A reporter I know, assigned to his station's investigative unit, discovered that a medical lab suspected of slipshod work was owned in part by one of his old school friends. To his credit, the reporter did not let this fact affect his work. But he had to deal with reproach, then anger, from his old friend, and of course lost the man's friendship.

CHAPTER 3

The Reporter's Tool Kit

You can always spot the radio reporter in a crowd: the one who walks with a list to one side because of the bag of *stuff* hanging on one shoulder. This chapter deals with what needs to be in that bag and what doesn't. What follows is mostly suggestions, with precious few commandments.

1. *Your mind.* Without curiosity, presence of mind and a developed ability to retain numerous facts in your short-term memory, all the other items are useless. A reporter with intelligence and intellectual discipline can have all of his or her belongings washed away in a flood, and return to the studio to give an informative, accurate and ear-grabbing report.

2. *Paper.* Many reporters find it convenient to take several sheets of paper, fold them in thirds like a letter going into an envelope, and stuff them into a pocket when going to a story. I find the special reporter's notebooks available from some larger stationery houses more versatile. The size, four by eight inches, fits nicely into a pocket, purse or bag. The lines are wide-spaced to accommodate the typical reporter's rapid scrawl.

And they can be propped over the steering wheel of a mobile unit for feeding from the field. Some reporters prefer steno notebooks or even legal pads. But by all means, carry some kind of paper. Life isn't a series of news conferences with nicely printed handouts to work from.

3. *Pens.* Take your choice, but take at least two. I like to pair a regular ballpoint with a fiber-tipped pen. The fiber-tip is useful for blocking out any part of typed copy I don't plan to read on the air. A series of X's doesn't do as thorough a job. And when doing pieces from the field, especially at night, the bold line of the fiber-tip is a lot easier to read. But the ink runs badly in the rain.

4. *Cassette recorder.* The brand and model aren't crucial, but it should be solidly constructed, easy to use and capable of high-quality sound. That leaves out the $29.95 cheapies, super-tiny dictating units and the AM-FM combos. You or your station can pay up to $800 for a super-duper recorder, and even more for one of the newer digital units. I normally carry two recorders, each purchased at Radio Shack for about $70. Some of the higher priced units have large XLR-style mike jacks, instead of mini-jacks which don't grip plugs very firmly. One expensive model has no loudspeaker: compact but less flexible. Most recorders come with automatic gain control (AGC), which is usually a good thing. But it's nice to have an AGC-defeat switch. That's the one marked "Voice-Music." "Voice" means the AGC is on, building up weak sounds and limiting the extra-loud ones. "Music" turns the AGC off, and avoids the sometimes-annoying buildup of background sounds during pauses. It helps if your recorder has both Mic (low level) and Line (high level) inputs. All models have mic-level inputs. The line-level input allows you to patch into other recorders, into public address systems, and into some "mult boxes" (multiple-outlet audio feed units), although most mult boxes have plenty of mic-level jacks. A Pause control is virtually necessary for feeding wraps from the field. A variable speed control can help save a tape if the batteries are becoming weak. Recorders that use larger cells, "C" or "D" size, need new batteries less often than those which operate on "AA" cells. The

voice-operated feature (VOX) found on some recorders is of no value to radio reporters, and should always be left in the "off" position.

5. *Microphone.* The built-in mic in your recorder is of limited use for radio. An external mic is a virtual necessity. A cheapie plastic mic is a false economy. Microphone selection and use is covered in Chapter Four.

6. *Pop screen.* That's the foam ball that goes over the head of the mic, to soften voice pops and reduce the whooshing sound you get on windy days. Most good professional mics have a pop screen built in. But feel free to add one.

7. *Mic stand.* It should point the mic upward toward the speaker, be stable so as not to topple over, and be compact (preferably folding.) A few plastic stands do the job, but may be so light that they become top-heavy when the mic is attached. Desk stands with cast metal bases are cumbersome to carry, and may not fit in when other mics are jammed onto a lectern.

8. *Goosenecks, clamps, etc.* Lots of accessories are available. Each has a use, but it may not come up very often. The most important single microphone accessory is gaffer's tape, discussed elsewhere in this chapter.

9. *Mic cords.* One is not enough. Varieties of mic cords are covered in Chapter Four.

10. *Change.* I'm not kidding. Unless your city or town has no pay phones or parking meters, you're well advised to stash some change in the bottom of your bag. If you work in a city with a mass transit system, some spare tokens or a farecard are also appropriate.

11. *Gaffer's tape.* There are two kinds of reporters in the field: those who carry gaffer's tape, and those who have to borrow it. See details this chapter.

12. *Alligator clips.* Most radio reporters use alligator clips, at least occasionally. The term applies to a commercially-available cord with a mini-plug on one end and a pair of spring-loaded clips on the other (Radio Shack 42–2421.) It is

used to feed sound from your recorder through the telephone, using either the two screw terminals on the back of the earphone or the two spring-metal contacts behind the mouthpiece. (This applies only to standard phones, whose plastic handset caps can be unscrewed.) The clips can also be attached to the bare leads of a broadcast loop, and the mini-plug inserted into the earphone jack, to use your recorder as a simple remote amplifier. Or a mini-to-mini patch cord can be created by clipping together two sets of alligator clips.

13. *Patch cords.* There are two kinds: regular and attenuating. The regular cord is used for feeding line-level sound into your recorder's line input, if it has one, or mic level sound into the mic input. It is also used to feed sound from the headphone jack into some telephone interface devices, such as the Voice-Act or Microtel. The attenuating patch cord has resistors built into the plugs, whose barrels are somewhat larger than regular. This cord automatically reduces the volume of whatever it feeds, and is used in the field to dub from the headphone jack of one recorder to the mic input of another recorder. Another term for this cord is a "dub cord" (Radio Shack 42–2152.)

14. *Other tape feed devices.* Telephones are wonderful things, found almost everywhere. But feeding tape, and especially wraps, over telephones so that something intelligible comes out the other end is a problem. Among devices for doing so are the alligator clips described above, an amplified screw-on attachment sold under the name Voice-Act, a tiny loudspeaker sold by Shure as its Acoustic Coupler, and electronic devices ranging from $250 to as much as $1,800. Gentner Electronics makes a compact and inexpensive unit called the Microtel, which I find useful.

15. *Extension cords.* Depending on the kinds of assignments you cover, you may want to have a twelve-foot AC cord from the hardware store. A mic extension cord is also useful, as described in Chapter Four.

16. *AC adapter.* If you find yourself frequently working out of a press room, your home or some other indoor location, you can save battery drain by carrying (or storing at

that location) an AC adapter designed for your recorder. Make sure the voltage is correct for your machine. A nine-volt adapter might "fry" a six-volt recorder. The adapter is a life-saver if your batteries die before you have a chance to feed your story to the station.

17. *Spares.* If you don't carry spare batteries, you deserve whatever happens to you (and it will, sooner or later.) This is especially true with recorders that use AA-size batteries, which have a shorter life than C- or D-size. You can go a year without needing a spare cassette tape, but you'll be glad to have one the day your machine eats the cassette in use, or an important meeting runs longer than sixty minutes. Some hardy—or cautious—types carry a spare recorder and/or mic. I do. I earn my living doing this. Excuses do not generate income. (But I recall the day a colleague discovered that he had a bad mic cord and reached triumphantly into his bag for his spare, only to learn that it, too, was bad.)

18. *Earphone.* Those little crystal earphones that come with recorders and transistor radios weigh next to nothing and allow you to monitor recording quality. If there's a problem, you can take corrective action promptly. You can also listen to your tape in a crowded room without bothering other people or letting competitors hear something exclusive.

19. *Transistor radio.* A small, inexpensive radio can be a big help when you're away from the news car. You can hear cues for live feeds, follow other reporters who may be covering other aspects of a major breaking story, or monitor the competition.

20. *Beeper.* Feel like a doctor (or crack dealer.) Never be out of touch with the newsroom. But make sure the desk uses restraint, and doesn't beep you on a minor pretext while you're in a major meeting, news conference or trial. Judges in particular look with disfavor on beepers going off in their courtrooms. Some beepers can be switched to operate silently, displaying a message on a tiny LCD screen.

21. *Flashlight.* For power outages, going places at night, even finding stuff in the bottom of your bag. A two-cell

penlight, or one of the tiny ones that uses a single cell, will do nicely. Pick one that won't turn on just by being jostled by other gear.

22. *Spare car keys.* You haven't locked yourself out of the news car yet? I have. Twice.

23. *Dogtag chain.* Most days, no one asks to see your press credentials. Occasionally, as at fires or visits by major national figures, it's a good idea to have ID's hanging around your neck. Electric light pull chain from the hardware store is good.

24. *Walkie-talkie or cellular phone.* The ultimate umbilical cord: great for live reports, but expensive. Audio quality is so-so, and you are subject to "dead spots" where transmission fails. The competition may listen in on your walkie-talkie. A CB transceiver cannot legally be used for the same purposes. Special high-quality PU units by Marti and others are sometimes used, where distances are not great.

25. *Scanner.* Of course there's one in the newsroom. There's probably one in the car. But if you cover much police and fire news, a pocket scanner may be worth the price.

26. *Something to carry all this gear in.* It will be a rare reporter who will find it worth carrying everything on this list. How light you travel is up to your own coverage needs. In the past, I have used a small gym bag, an attache case, even my pockets. In recent years, I have used a shoulder bag from the luggage department of a discount store. Many reporters use camera bags, which have lots of pockets, but tend to be expensive, and often include superfluous padding. I've seen tote bags, backpacks, canvas brief cases and large purses used. Evolve something that works for you through trial (careful) and error (as little as possible).

Gaffer's Tape

The following had its genesis one afternoon in Boston City Hall. I went to a pay phone to feed in a wrap, and found myself facing one of those flush-mount jobbies, with no horizontal space above or below the phone. Okay, set the bag on the floor, hold the recorder in the right hand, hold the phone in the left hand, and . . . . how would I hold my notebook so that I could read the script?

After a moment, the little light bulb above my head lit up, and I reached into my bag for that indispensible roll of gaffer's tape. I tore off a piece about three inches long to attach the whole notebook to the brick wall next to the phone, and a little piece about the size of a thumbnail to hold the page I was going to turn, since the script jumped to a second page.

Gaffer's tape, for those who aren't in the habit of carrying it, is a gray cloth-based tape, very sticky but capable of being peeled off of most surfaces without damage. And you can tear it with your hands. It's generally sold in hardware stores, where it's frequently called duct (or "duck") tape. It usually comes in rolls two inches wide. Lengths vary, but the shorter rolls are a lot easier to carry than the jumbo economy size. Mystic brand cloth tape is somewhat similar, and can be used for some of the same purposes. But the real thing is worth hunting for. Anything the local transit authority can use to hold old streetcars together, even as I attach a notebook to a brick wall, has got to be good stuff.

How versatile, you may ask, is gaffer's tape? Let us count the ways:

1. *Mount a microphone on a lectern.* Use a piece to firmly mount the mic to the top of the lectern, or a couple of smaller pieces to keep the legs of a folding mic stand from sliding down the sloping copy surface of the lectern. Or attach the mic to someone else's mike already firmly mounted on the lectern.

2. *Mount mics on a stand.* A standard practice at many news conferences in open spaces is that one TV photog will contribute a light stand. Then with lots of gaffer's tape and no little ingenuity, everybody's mic is taped to the top of the stand. You don't leave until everybody else leaves.

3. *Attach a mic to a PA speaker.* You may arrive late, or the facility may be so designed that you just can't put your

microphone atop the lectern—or there may be several people speaking, panel-style. You can use a largish piece of tape to stick your mic to the grille cloth of a public address speaker, as outlined in Chapter Four.

4. *Attach a cassette recorder to a mic stand.* Not real common, but I recall an event at which a mic stand was in the middle of a large stage. I didn't have an extension mic cord, my recorder was very compact, and I had advance access to the stage. Plenty of drawbacks, not the least of which is that once you start the recorder, it runs, and you have no access to it until the event is over.

5. *Safety protection for long cords.* Convenience is sitting in a chair fifteen feet from the lectern, recorder on one's lap, taking notes with tape counter numbers included. Embarrassment is having someone trip over one's extension mic cord. So one peels off pieces several feel long and tapes said cord to the floor. Being a frugal sort, I hate throwing away twelve feet of tape at the end of the event, but some things are made to be discarded.

6. *Hold your equipment together.* Good enough for the transit authority, good enough for me. Lose the cover to your battery compartment? Okay, replace it with gaffer's tape. Reinforce worn spots on the recorder's carrying case or shoulder strap. I've even used the stuff to cover a broken-out record-protect tab on an audio cassette.

7. *The old notebook-on-the-wall trick.*

8. *Mark workspace boundaries.* Example: one table is provided for several stations to use at an event. Okay, "Good fences make good neighbors." A narrow strip keeps you and the reporter from WXXX from becoming testy when things get busy.

9. *Labelling.* The tape can be written on. Use small pieces to label inputs on your mixer at a remote, or the filing number you're to call from the election headquarters, or (See 8. above) label your staked-out workspace.

10. *Make friends.* Your colleague/competitor can use gaffer's tape for all the same things you can. But he/she didn't bring any. So you generously produce a roll from your bag and peel off a couple of inches/feet/yards. Cheaper than a box of doughnuts, and just as sticky.

11. *Keep the news car going.* This list originally had ten uses for gaffer's tape, but my wife reminds me that it's also waterproof—worth remembering, should you suffer a broken radiator hose on your way to an event.

CHAPTER 4

Microphone Technique

Microphone Basics

The microphone is the radio reporter's indispensable tool: it is the ear through which the audience hears everything he or she does. And how well the reporter uses the microphone determines how effectively that work reaches the audience. The neophyte often thinks that the mic hears the way the human ear/brain combination does. It doesn't, so we have to compensate. The ear is essentially omnidirectional, and has a matching ear located on the other side of the head to help out. The head conveniently swivels on the neck to optimize pickup. And the brain does a remarkable job of filtering out distracting sounds or echoes. Nobody has built a mic that does all these things.

Microphones are designed for specific applications. The variables include directional pickup, frequency response, dynamic range, and shock resistance. Models are available at prices ranging from less than ten dollars to more than two thousand dollars. The cheap ones lack the sound quality and durability needed for broadcast use. The expensive ones are either intended for critical studio work or are highly specialized designs. This chapter will focus on durable, general-purpose designs of moderate cost. A radio reporter has little need of a mic with a broad dynamic range, capable of withstanding extremely high sound levels, such as those used by rock singers. Of greater importance are directional characteristics.

Many microphones are "omnidirectional." This means that they pick up sound from all directions. However, there are limits to the accuracy of that statement. An omnidirectioal mic isn't very good at picking up sound from behind it or even very far off axis. To understand "axis", think of the mic as a fencer's foil. The blade represents the mic's axis. All microphones pick up optimally along that axis. The omnidirectional design is most tolerant of sounds coming from off to one side or another. Several manufacturers offer sturdy, high-quality omnidirectional microphones at reasonable prices. A leading example is the Electro-Voice 635A.

Another common microphone design is "cardioid." A graph of its response looks something like a heart, hence the name. Its pattern "attenuates" or diminishes the strength of off-axis sound more than does the omnidirectional design. This is a good mic for field work, because it tends not to pick up undesired peripheral sound, such as traffic or airplanes. At the same time, it is tolerant of a certain amount of bad aim by the person using it. Newsrooms on tight budgets take note: Radio Shack's model 33–984 provides good cardioid pickup for about sixty dollars.

Most directional of all are the "shotgun" microphones used by many TV crews. They are unsuitable for general use, but nice to have in the news car when certain occasions arise. A subspecies of this design is the "noise-cancelling" microphone, which is highly directional, but does not pick up sound from a great distance. If you carry one, use it when there is a great deal of distracting noise nearby. It's fine for interviewing someone near a jackhammer, but so effective that a report from a parade would lose its impact, because the marching bands would be virtually inaudible.

It should be noted that the attenuation of off-axis sound by a microphone is not constant across the frequency specturum. The frequencies that drop off first tend to be highs. That is why we speak of off-mic voices as sounding "mushy."

Frequency response is important in choosing a microphone. It is usually expressed in this fashion: 60–15,000 Hz. Such a mic will reliably pick up sounds between these frequencies, but response drops off beyond those points. High frequency response makes for a "crisp" sound; poor highs make a mic sound dull or mushy. Low frequencies provide body; without good low-frequency response, a mic sounds tinny. But too strong a low-frequency response can make a mic sound "boomy," a poor choice for outdoor use.

Most microphones have a different frequency response to sounds originating very close to them. A voice will sound more natural if the mic is placed from five inches to a foot away, than if just an inch or two away. Additionally, if you mic a speaker too closely, there is an increased liklihood that the automatic gain control (AGC) in your recorder will have to work harder to keep the sound within acceptable limits. When the AGC has to clamp down too hard, the result is less natural-sounding. (The "proximity effect" produced by speaking very close to a mic emphasizes low frequencies. For this reason, many studio announcers like to work very close to the mic, to make their voices sound deeper.)

Figure 1

Frequency response curve for common omnidirectional microphone. Courtesy of Electro-Voice, Inc.

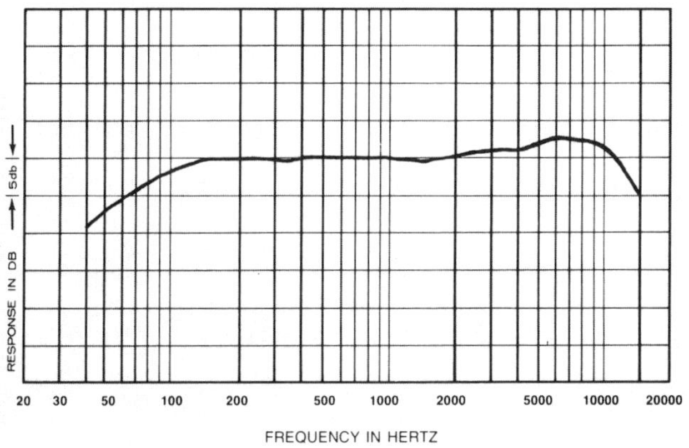

FIGURE 1 — Response Curve

Figure 2

Diagrams of pickup sensitivity for typical omnidirectional and cardioid microphones. Courtesy of Shure Brothers Inc.

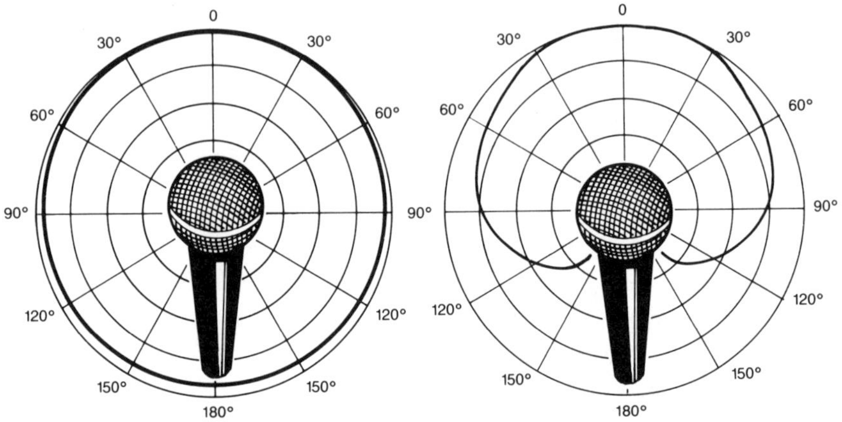

Polar pattern diagrams for typical omnidirectional and unidirectional (cardioid) microphones

Microphone Placement

How should the radio reporter apply the information just outlined? First, you should now realize that just having the microphone somewhere near the speaker will not do the job. It should be reasonably close to the speaker, and pointed toward his or her mouth. In interview situations, that means about six inches from the speaker's chin, low enough not to block a photographer's shot, but with the axis coming close to the speaker's mouth. Too far away, and you get poor frequency response or extraneous sound on tape; too close and you risk losing quality to the proximity effect (and suffering the embarrassment of hitting the speaker in the mouth.) Beginners: don't be bashful! Get in close with the "pros" for good sound.

When placing a mic on a lectern or table, use a stand. Laying the mike down flat not only means that the speaker will be off-axis, but you'll probably get dandy pickup of shuffling papers or a fist hitting the lectern for emphasis. When recording a band, point the axis away from the squealing clarinets to favor the mid-range trombones or saxophones, but avoid drums, whose brief but loud percussive sounds can give an AGC fits.

When working outdoors, move the microphone to keep loud trucks, sirens or passing jet planes off-axis. When recording your own voice in the field, keep the mike as far from your own mouth as you do from anyone else's (perhaps a tad farther, if you speak louder than non-broadcasters) to avoid falling victim to the proximity effect.

Accessories

If the microphone is a professional model, it comes with a built-in connector, usually of the three-pin XLR design. It's wise to carry two cords: a six-foot cord for interviews and podium use, and a fifteen-to-twenty-five-foot extension for meetings and some kinds of news conferences. I find it convenient to carry a third cord, only two or three feet long, for one-on-ones, so as not to have unneeded cord dangling as I walk. The long cord allows you to put your mic up at a meeting or news conference and hold the recorder in your lap, starting or stopping as seems appropriate. This reduces the amount of tape you have to go through afterward. (If one cord should go bad, usually indicating the need to re-solder a connection, you can make do with one of the others.)

Some reporters prefer to use, in place of the shorter cord, a coiled cord made from a stereo headphone extension, available in electronics stores. It is only a few feet long in its normal state—good for interviews—but stretches to twelve or more feet when needed. The one pitfall is that when stretched out, the cord's tension may pull it out of the jack in your recorder. A strip of gaffer's tape will anchor it safely.

Some kind of stand is certainly advisable. As noted earlier, a mic lying directly on a lectern or table will not provide optimum pickup. A mic stand need not be of the heavy cast-metal variety. Folding or collapsable stands are available, notably the AKG model 231, which lists for under ten dollars. In the absence of a stand, you can use strips of gaffer's tape to attach your mic to someone else's stand. One drawback of this practice is that you must wait until the event is over to remove your mic, while a mic on its own stand can sometimes be fished out of the cluster of stands for an early departure. In an extreme case, you could use gaffer's tape to attach your recorder itself (providing it's a pocket model) to a mic stand, if you have no cord.

There are times when a microphone cannot be placed before the speaker. Examples include panel-type news conferences or board meetings, when each of several speakers has his or her own mic, or occasions when you show up late and the event is already underway. If a multiple-outlet (mult) box is provided, you will be able to plug in, using your mic cord. Absent a mult box, you may be able to plug into the house sound system, using an attentuating patch cord. Or you may have to resort once again to your roll of gaffer's tape to attach your mic to the front of the public address speaker. The results of this last tactic will range from adequate to awful.

If you find yourself frequently covering stories at which a group of reporters crowd together (example: defendants or lawyers emerging from courtrooms or elevators,) you may want to use a telescoping "fishpole" boom. Extendable models are available commercially. You can build one in an hour with a piece of aluminum conduit tubing from the hardware store, a bicycle handlebar grip on one end and a spare mic clamp on the other. A leg cut off a collapsible photographic tripod can also be converted into an extendable fishpole. Be warned that such an accessory, while useful, can be a nuisance to carry around, and is easily left behind.

Moving People

And, if all else fails, and mic placement doesn't do the trick, you can resort to people placement. Example A: an organization calls a news conference with five people seated side-by-side. Each plans to speak from his or her position. Your courteous explanation that you want all of them to be heard clearly by the folks at home may motivate them to play "musical chairs," each occupying the center seat (the one behind the cluster of mics) in turn. Example B: Somebody holds a news conference, standing behind a lectern on which the microphones are located. He or she walks away in the middle of the statement to point to something on a chart, or refers a question to an associate standing several feet away. It really is possible to speak up politely, asking the speaker to step to the microphone. It takes a lot of nerve, but it works.

CHAPTER 5

Interviewing

The most basic technique in gathering news (beyond ripping it off the wire) is interviewing. Whether calling the police and fire stations on our morning rounds, or pressing a presidential candidate on a global issue, we ask questions to get information. And the way we craft those questions determines in large part how much information we get, and how useful it is.

Broadcast reporters have an additional factor to keep in mind: we need not only facts to scribble down, but also usable sound bites. So our questions must be put with greater care than a print reporter can get away with. Further, we must keep in mind the amount of time available to us. Let's look at three general types of interviews, for illustration.

THE QUICKIE: The defendant's lawyer is emerging from the courtroom after the jury returns its verdict, or the mayor is about to get into his/her car, or the fire chief takes a quick break during a three-alarmer. Time is of the essence. You do not have the luxury of laying the groundwork with preliminary questions. What is the *one* thing you most want to know?

How did the verdict square with the evidence? What will you do now that city council has defeated your incinerator plan? How much of a threat is the fire to the surrounding neighborhood?

Questions which can easily be answered "yes" or "no" may be answered just that way, and should be avoided. If the subject is willing to hold still for a few more seconds, you can get in a second or even a third question. Again, keep the questions very much to the point, and listen closely to what is said, to see if you can use it as a bite. If the answer is disjointed, but the information is important, say something like, "I'm afraid I don't understand", in hopes that the subject will rephrase the answer. One thing to bear in mind during such an interview is that your time sense is probably distorted. What seems like a nice long answer may in fact be only four or five seconds. So, even though it may seem gratuitous, going after that second or third or fourth question is usually a good idea.

THE BASIC Q & A: It may be following an evening meeting, it may be an interview on the phone, or it may be somebody from the United Way who stops by the station. But the assumption is that you have three or four minutes, and can develop the interview to some extent. Such an interview might go like this:

- What is the problem at hand?
- What proposals exist for dealing with it?
- What obstacles must be overcome?
- What steps will you take to do that?
- What is the next thing you will now do?

Each of those generic questions has the potential for yielding a useful actuality or two. But in this type of interview, you have the luxury of asking a "fishing" question, with no certainty of the answer being useful. As with the Quickie interview, if you hear a good point being made, but inadequately, ask a question that covers the same ground, such as, "Tell me that again—that's very interesting." And, since you may have not only the next few newscasts to worry about, but also tomorrow morning, or the weekend, a question or two that look toward the future can extend the life of the story by providing a next-day lead.

THE LONG-FORM INTERVIEW: If the Quickie places demands on the reporter for conciseness, the Long-Form Interview puts a premium on filling the time at hand. Typically, the setting is the weekend public-affairs show, or perhaps a daily talk show, with or without call-ins from the public. I once worked for a small talk-formatted station in the dual role of news director and talk show host. I was responsible for the local newscasts which preceded each of my two consecutive hours of talk. Thus, I seldom met the guest for the first hour before going on the air, and never met the guest for the second hour before air time. We had the length of the network newscast to become acquainted. Larry King says he prefers to ask questions to which he does not know the answers. I had no choice. So the first few questions were intended to define the guest, both for the listener and for myself. There were no quick jumps. We proceeded at a very deliberate pace. If I didn't have a lot of unanswered questions in mind as we passed the half-hour point, I worried. The "what do you do next?" questions didn't get asked until around :45. And I became adept at spotting possible ramifications: "Well, if you do that, how will it affect X?"

The foregoing may sound elementary, but I recall the day when a skilled reporter at a major Boston station interviewed a woman just elected to public office, who was, shall we say, a model of taciturnity. A page of typed questions was consumed in the first ten minutes. The show was haif an hour. The reporter remembers it to this day as the worst half-hour of her career.

Here are some pointers in doing any of these interviews, if the real reason is to get sound bites for newscasts (which is usually the case): Don't worry about micing yourself, unless you realize that the subject is so tongue-tied that your questions will be needed to make the sound hang together. Let a half-second pass before you ask the next question, to make your editing job a little easier. Try to steer your subject away from dated answers that use words like "tonight" or "tomorrow", unless you only plan to use the sound in the next couple of hours. Avoid questions that can be answered with a word or two; use qualitative questions, such as "How will this affect . . .?" And if you see a way to move the overall story beyond what you got in a news release or the newspaper, by all means do so.

Asking Questions

Press conferences present a unique setting for questioning newsmakers. Reporters from different media, numbering from a handful to scores, jointly ask questions, with few guiding rules. Each reporter has his or her own needs. Radio reporters need two things: facts and sound. If all we needed were facts, we might ask questions in the choppy way that many print reporters do, interrupting answers as soon as the desired information is given, to jump to the next question. Like our television colleagues, we prefer complete sentences without other voices overlapping. Unlike our video siblings, we must come up with sound for a series of essentially duplicative newscasts. Most radio wraps are shorter than most TV packages. Lacking visual context, we need cuts which are clearly audible and whose meaning can easily be understood. So here is an admittedly arbitrary list of valid reasons for asking questions:

1. To get basic information, whether on tape or not. (How did this accident happen?)

2. To get usable actualities. (Tell me what the fire looked like as the first units arrived.)

3. To get usable duplicate actualities, for the following hour's newscast. (Really? A teachers' strike? Is that what you're saying?)

4. To clarify a point. (You said "take action"; just what kind of action?)

5. To get fuller detail. (What are some of the recommendations in your report?)

6. Or on the other hand, to get a more concise answer. (That's a pretty long list. Can you sum up what you want to achieve?)

7. To provoke the newsmaker to speak more candidly. (I don't know much about "enforcement implementation under Section 21(a)." Is that a lot like throwing the book at them?)

8. To fill a gap left by other reporters' questions. (So far, we haven't gotten to what happens if the funding falls through. Can you address that for us?)

9. To confirm what you have been told unofficially or have reason to believe. (I've been hearing something about an employee of the bank being arrested. What can you tell me about that?)

There is no rule, by the way, that keeps you from following up an unresponsive answer with a polite "All of that doesn't really answer the question I asked. Would you do that, please?" Nothing except your fear that the newsmaker might get mad at you. Too bad; ask anyway. If he or she does get mad, the experience will be educational.

You will notice that the sample questions above are of the essay variety. Questions that can be answered yes or no invite just that. Ask "How upset are you?", not "Are you upset?"

I advise caution when asking questions that put words in the newsmaker's mouth, and even more caution when writing up the response. (The preceding sentence is in the first person because some reporters use the technique successfully, and would bristle at the suggestion that it's poor journalism. I just think it steers newsmakers too much.) In one celebrated incident, a candidate had said repeatedly that he believed that he could deal with a state deficit without raising taxes. One reporter persisted, "But is that a lead-pipe guarantee?" The candidate, slightly annoyed, answered "Yes!" The phrase "lead-pipe guarantee" appeared in a front page headline the following morning, in quotes. For years afterward, most people thought the candidate had spoken the words unprompted.

If you choose to toss out a phrase to see if the newsmaker accepts it, I would urge you to write, "When asked if he was making a lead-pipe guarantee, Smith responded 'yes' ". Writing "Smith said he's making a lead-pipe guarantee" just isn't factual. In radio, this might be the time to include your question in the actuality, so that the listener understands who is choosing which words. Merely agreeing with a word or phrase is far different from uttering it.

Just as there are valid reasons for asking questions, there are invalid ones. Here are a few:

1. To show how much you know. Nobody cares if you know all about car insurance or fighting fires or the workings of the county school district. And there is the possibility that you don't know as much as you think you do, and it shows.

2. To debate a point or argue with the newsmaker. You're working for the public, not for your ego. If it's all that important to show the newsmaker to be wrong, take out nomination papers and run for his or her office.

3. To "show the colors." Some reporters attending news conferences think they haven't done their jobs until they have piped up with a question. Nobody keeps score. What counts is the story you file.

4. To get your voice into the actuality. At a few very large stations, reporters are paid fees for voicers, wraps and Q&A's. So there's a temptation to throw a quick but superfluous question into the middle of a one-on-one answer.

5. To satisfy your curiosity. Granted, native curiosity is a trait common to most reporters. But questions with that motivation alone slow down a news conference or group interview. On the other hand, if you're doing a one-on-one interview, and the interviewee has scheduled some time for it, questions beyond those needed for the story at hand may be in order.

A reporter should use caution in timing questions during news conferences. A clear dynamic often develops, and several reporters may center on a specific subtopic before things move on. Listen before asking a question. The late Steve Flanders of WCBS-AM, a top-flight reporter, once told me of a news conference at which a public official was trying to duck questions on a particular point, and several reporters were jointly pressing the issue—until another reporter obliviously jumped in with an entirely unrelated question, getting the evasive official off the hook. The reporter narrowly missed being drawn and quartered on the spot.

Getting the Most from Your Tape

How often does this happen? You get into the news car, drive to an event, record a person or persons, go back to the station, and pull off only two or three cuts. I suspect a fair number of people will respond that that's what they usually do, and wonder why I act as if there's something wrong with it.

Actually, there's nothing *wrong* with it, but under some circumstances, it's inefficient. Each time you press the "record" button, you are going into a mine for a basic raw material: sound. To emerge from the mine with only enough coal for tonight's fire is to leave your supplies low tomorrow. The idea is to bring out of that mine all the raw material you can find. Here are some examples:

An important public official speaks at a local college. You find the speech pretty dull. You can make a story out of it, of course, but nothing special. So you grab said public official afterward, and ask him or her to go into some detail on some portion of the speech that you found reasonably promising. It's just possible that, freed of the formal circumstances of talking to a large gathering, he/she will loosen up and say something more interesting. You ask a question that looks to the future: what's next, when will the report be ready, how soon will legislation be filed, or some such. If the official does come up with a point you consider newsworthy, get him/her to give you a second usable cut by asking for clarification. And if all this doesn't work, scan your memory of the issues of the day for one or two that are in the official's province, and ask for a comment. Ask the mayor about the new state projection of economic growth—is the local picture better or worse? Ask the State Senator whether the education reform bill passed yesterday will produce results in the coming school year. And so on. A good three-minute interview could produce as many as four cuts on one, two or even three topics—if you're lucky.

The president of the local electric company holds a news conference on the environmental impact of some new transmission line towers. When that topic is exhausted, pipe up with the reporter's favorite transition: "On another topic, Mr. Kilowatt . . ." He's there in front of you, so tap his expertise and newsworthiness. How are falling world oil prices being reflected in this utility's bills? Will the court suit challenging construction of the nuclear power plant in the neighboring state have any effect on local power supply or prices? Try not to be too far-fetched, but do consider logical topic linkages.

You tape the City Council meeting as they discuss the purchase of three new police cars. Your lead, of course, will be the purchase of the cars (or rejection of the purchase, if that's the vote). But along the way, the police chief says that one of the present cars almost had an accident last week, because its brakes are shot, or the cops are complaining that their cars are in worse shape than the ones they stop for having bad mufflers. There's your sidebar. Not the top of the story, perhaps, but the listener may relate to it more directly.

What to do with these additional sound bites? After you've pulled the basic cuts for your wraps, pull others for use in newscasts that don't use your wraps. Hold some til tomorrow morning. If today's Thursday, do up a couple of weekenders. Holiday weekend coming up? This has got to be better than tracking the fatality toll.

Here's another way to make tape work harder: The newsmaker makes the bulk of his or her points in just two or three paragraphs/statements/answers. You observe that one statement runs 32 seconds, and is repetitious about a point. Instead of using the basic 18 seconds for your wrap, and ignoring the rest, perhaps there's a nine-second mini-bite in the outtake that would go nicely in your wrap (the boss has commented that some of your wraps were running too long, anyway). Then you save the 18-second cut for use in a different newscast. Do that a couple of times, and what had looked like barely enough tape becomes two wraps and two spare cuts.

Never forget that the tape that you put on the air should be clear and informative, but use your imagination to find ways to use as much of it as possible, in ways that are not immediately obvious.

The Dreaded MOS

The "man on the street" (or "person in parking lot") is one of the least favorite assignments of many reporters. On paper, MOS is an attractive form of reporting, in that it produces short actualities of real people commenting on the day's events. For a moment, the listener is delivered from elected officials, press spokespeople and other "usual suspects." In our egalitarian society, "real people" are presumed to have authentic opinions untainted by power or position. So we seek out the man/woman on the street.

The problem is that the person on the street may not want to be sought out, and when corralled, may not have anything much to say or much coherence to his or her thoughts. The reporter on an MOS assignment can come to feel as if he or she is peddling leprosy, or stumbling upon graduates of the State School For the Bewildered. The good news is that there are steps the reporter can take to improve the experience all around.

Timing is important. Seeking public reaction too soon after an event can produce a lot of blank stares. I recall being sent onto the sidewalks of Manhattan less than half an hour after Nelson Rockefeller resigned as Governor of New York. No one I approached had heard the news, and few had any opinion to offer on short notice.

Some locations are better than others. In Boston, reporters are often sent to the centrally-located Park Street subway station for MOS. My experience is that people at such places are often in a hurry to get somewhere, and don't feel they have the time to spend answering questions. I've had good luck on the sidewalk near convenience stores, or in shopping center parking lots.

The nature of the story may dictate the best location for getting MOS comment. If the story has to do with politics, the best hunting may be near a public building, such as City Hall. Consumer issues can be pursued in a major shopping area. Entertainment issues might best be taken to a ticket agency or record store.

How the reporter approaches a member of the public has a lot to do with whether the person agrees to be interviewed. Here are some rules I follow:

1. Try not to seem to swoop down on the person. People become apprehensive when they see a stranger zeroing in on them from a distance. Walking too quickly can set off alarm bells.

2. Avoid threatening body language. I keep my hands out of my pockets, avoid holding the microphone toward the person before speaking, and smile (but not too broadly.) And I don't approach too closely before making my intentions known.

3. Introduce yourself in as few words as possible, and try not to sound canned. "Hi, I'm Mary Snerd of WXXX, and I'm asking people about the new landfill proposal. Do you have a few seconds?" I would counsel against sounding pushy or self-important. A little self-deprecation can help. I frequently tell prospects who appear to be older than 40 that I'm "pestering" people about issue X. Tailor your technique not only to your prospect, but to yourself. Things that work well for a middle-aged man may not work well for a younger reporter or one who is female.

4. Don't just plow into the first question without getting some kind of assent, be it verbal or in the form of body language.

5. Learn to distinuish between a flat refusal and mere reticence. There's no sense pressing, if a private or timid person says "no comment." But some people just need reassurance that they won't make fools of themselves. Radio reporters are sometimes told "I don't want to be on TV." Bear in mind that there are people out there who do not realize that a camera is

necessary for television. TV is magic. You have a microphone. Therefore, you must be from TV. My response, which usually works, is, "Oh, this is better than TV—it's radio. Nobody can see you; they'll just hear what you have to say."

Once your subject has agreed to be interviewed, phrase the questions so that they contain information about the topic. "Do you think the Mayor is doing the right thing by trying to cut three percent from the school budget?" helps to define the issue. Determine from the response to your opening question whether to keep your followups broad ("What would you rather see done about school spending?") or focussed ("What do you think will happen if fifteen teachers are laid off?") Questions that cannot be answered "yes" or "no" usually produce more useful answers.

Your questions should not indicate partisanship. Nor should they seem to pass judgement on answers your subject has already given. Your subject may be looking for clues to the kind of answers you "want" to hear.

If you're planning to edit responses into a montage, you should try to ask your subjects essentially the same questions, so that the people your audience hear juxtaposed one to another are all talking about the same thing.

If you want or need the subject's name, wait until after the interview, when the person will presumably be more at ease. Keep it non-threatening. "Could I get your name and where you're from?" beats "What's your name and where do you live?" Accept refusals gracefully. If unsure about the spelling or pronunciation, ask the subject to make it clear on the tape.

Get more sound than you think you will need. What feels like plenty of good responses may turn out to be only three or four usable cuts, none over six seconds. While waiting for the next prospect, run the tape back to listen for poor audio quality, extraneous traffic sounds, and other elements that can kill an otherwise good interview. Before returning to the station, listen to the entire tape to make sure you have enough material.

And that's all there is to it. Follow these handy rules, and within a scant ten or twenty years, you may actually come to like doing MOS.

How NOT to Do MOS

The following was perpetrated by a colleague who will remain nameless. The racial tensions surrounding the Boston school busing crisis were at their peak one Saturday in the mid-1970's. A beach at what some considered the boundary between a neighborhood of largely militant whites and a large public housing project occupied predominantly by blacks had become a bone of contention. Blacks asserted a right to use the beach; whites vowed to resist them. Large groups of each were gathered on the beach, shouting and waving fists (or variants thereof.) A line of police kept the two angry groups apart, fearing that fighting might break out at any moment. Into this setting strode the journalist in question, carrying a cassette recorder and shouting out, "Press! Anyone want to be interviewed?" (The police escorted him to his car—quickly.)

CHAPTER 6

Voicers and Wraps

Radio reports—those incorporated into newscasts voiced by someone other than the reporter—are generally spoken of in terms of the forms they take. This chapter will deal with the two most common forms: the Voicer and the Wrap.

The Voicer is the simplest form of report. It consists of the reporter telling the story in his or her own voice, either in-studio or from the field. It is virtually always scripted, and ends with a Sign-off (sometimes called a Lockout.) The voicer embodies the same elements as a full-length story in a newscast: Lead, development and wrapup. But to avoid duplication, the first sentence is usually given to the anchor, and the reporter picks up with the second line (hence, the term "second-line lead" for this structure.) Let's analyze a script:

5/3/91 TEACHERS	Comments
Plans to lay off Boston school teachers are now in the hands of a judge. WXXX's John Doe reports: —more—	Anchor reads the lead. It's in present tense, because it tells where things stand right now.

—more—	
Suffolk Superior Court Judge Charles Barrett heard the Boston Teachers Union argue that the School Committee should be barred from laying off three hundred school teachers.	Reporter uses past tense, telling what happened in court. While this is a development sentence, it's heavy on "who-what-where."
Layoff notices went out today, and a vote on the layoffs is due at a special School Committee meeting late Monday afternoon at Madison Park High School.	This sentence was the lead earlier in the day. We're now updating it. Why name the school? The public may want to attend.
The BTU says the hasty layoffs violate due process. It wants, at the least, longer notice.	Summing court argument, first one side . . .
The School Committee says the teachers will have a chance—as a group—to try to persuade them not to go forward with the layoffs.	. . . then the other.
Judge Barrett is studying the case over the weekend and is expected to rule on Monday. The Teachers Union will spend the weekend prepping for that meeting.	Story ends with "what comes next" for both sides. (Weak wording here: "that meeting" refers to School Committee vote, not judge's ruling earlier the same day.)
At Suffolk Superior Court, John Doe, WXXX News.	Signoff places reporter at scene of event.

Usual practice is to keep the anchor's intro short, with only as much information as is needed to get into the voicer. Sometimes, however, the story is fairly complex, and the reporter is covering only part of it. In that case, the anchor may have a more fact-intensive lead, possibly running to more than one sentence. Other times, the anchor may merely tease the story ("Layoffs threaten Boston Schools"). In that case, the reporter's copy would begin with a classic lead sentence.

Some reporter pieces are "self-introed." Suppose a second reporter was working on the teacher layoff story, talking with teachers about the personal impact of layoffs. In that case, the first report might be followed by: "This is Jane Roe in Roslindale. Several teachers from the Zilch Middle School say they'll have a hard time paying their bills . . ."

Multiple-reporter packages may involve two other devices to unify the package. The anchor may follow the lead with, "We have two reports. First, John Doe." The reporter doing the first piece may then hand off to the second reporter, saying, ". . . I'm John Doe. The threat of layoffs worries some teachers. Jane Roe has that part of the story." Clearly, decisions about multi-reporter packages must be made far enough in advance for the reporters to produce pieces with the requisite intros and handoffs.

The voicer may be as brief or as lengthy as the story and station policy dictate. A voicer of less than twenty seconds —especially if several seconds are taken up with the signoff— can tell little more than a fragment of most stories. On the other hand, a report of more than forty or forty-five seconds is hard to fit into the three minutes or so of news within a five-minute newscast, without reducing story count. But news concerns itself with the exceptional, so it's a wise station whose policy allows for over-length reports when a story of sufficient impact or complexity comes along.

The Wrap

It comes in all shapes and sizes, but the wrap—or "V/A" for "voice-actuality"—is the chief product of radio reporters. By mixing the reporter's concise explanation of the story with an actuality—or "sound bite"—the listener is given a neutral account plus some "being there" flavor. But a reporter must avoid getting into a rut and doing all wraps according to the same cookie-cutter formula.

Let's begin by stating the formula:

- The anchor intro
- A lead sentence, setting up the story
- A development sentence, which leads into the actuality
- The actuality, whose context must be clear from the copy preceding it
- The wrapup sentence, to sweep up any loose facts

There may be three sentences leading into the actuality, if needed, or two following it. With this formula, we account for 95 percent of the wraps on radio.

Now, let's analyze a sample wrap, having to do with a fatal auto-pedestrian accident, in which a former member of the Boston Celtics was charged:

3/22/91 CELTICS/B-U	**Comments**
Anchor: Boston University President John Silber calls for improved traffic enforcement, in the wake of this morning's accident. WXXX's John Doe reports:	Wrap was preceded by hard top on the arraignment of the driver. Intro gets Silber's time-consuming title out of wrap copy.
Reporter: Dr. Silber says the entire B-U community is "shocked and saddened" by the deaths of An Tranh and Michelle Dartley.	Lead is in present tense because Silber presumably still feels this way.
He told reporters this afternoon that it's not a story about the Celtics or about B-U, but about reckless driving and pointless death:	Development sentence is in past tense because it refers to a specific event, the news conference from which actuality was drawn.
Actuality: Incue: "We will go through . . ." Outcue: ". . . go to work again."	Runs 13 seconds
Reporter: Silber noted that B-U has filed a bill with the legislature to allow its police to make traffic arrests along Commonwealth Avenue.	Wrapup looks forward (but fails to make clear whether bill was filed before the accident or because of it.)
At Boston University, John Doe, WXXX News.	Wrap was filed from news car in B-U parking lot.

The first three words of the wrapup sentence could have been dropped, since it is unlikely that there is any doubt as to whether the bill has been filed. But trimming those words would eliminate a back-identification of the actuality.

Time Limitations

Several factors dictate the structure of a wrap. Most fundamental is the amount of air time available. Many stations specify that a wrap may not exceed thirty, forty or forty-five seconds. Without arguing the wisdom of such strictures, it's clear that they impose a kind of discipline. At thirty seconds, the reporter is virtually compelled to put a lot of factual information into the anchor's lead-in, and start his or her own wrap with the second line of the story. Actualities are seldom as long as fifteen seconds—sometimes as brief as six or seven seconds. And it is sometimes not possible to include a wrapup sentence following the actuality. Some years ago, one network specified thirty-second wraps, and achieved this by having the actuality be the last element . . . the reporter did not sign off!

If the house limit is more generous, perhaps as long as forty-five seconds, an ingenious reporter can occasionally get two short actualities in, at least if the story is already familiar to the audience, which eliminates the reporter's need to explain the issue at hand. In any case, actualities should be carefully selected to avoid repetition. A two-sentence actuality running fifteen seconds or so may convey a significant amount of information. If the time limit is something greater than forty-five seconds, a reporter has more leeway to select sound, to describe an issue or an event, or even include a nuance or two.

News directors trying to keep story counts up might consider an alternative to a mandatory forty-second maximum (which tends also to become the minimum): encourage reporters to do certain stories in thirty seconds or less, thereby allowing the more complicated story to run closer to a minute.

Here are some stylistic tricks that can help deal with time limits:

1. Begin the wrap with actuality which contains substantial factual or emotional information in the first few seconds, then fade it under and do what is essentially a voicer from there on out.

2. Avoid redundancy in introducing sound:

Reporter: Mayor Smith says City Council doesn't understand the need for a balanced budget:

Actuality: "I keep telling Council that we've got to balance the budget, but they don't listen.'"

becomes "Mayor Smith responds:".

In some cases, simply introing the cut, "Mayor Smith:" will do. Omitting an intro altogether can be confusing even if the speaker is well known, and will leave the listener in a fog if the speaker is a private citizen or little-known minor official.

3. Use syntactic shorthand, such as a brief question in place of a lengthy declarative sentence:

> "Commissioner Jones says the next step is to begin an investigation, which he says could take as long as three months to complete."
>
> . . . *becomes* . . .
>
> "What's next? An investigation, taking up to three months."

Sentence fragments can be used, but are dangerous in the hands of an unskilled writer, who risks sounding illiterate.

The Nature of the Story

Running a strong second in determining the structure of a wrap is the nature of the story. A resourceful reporter does not write a story about clown day at the circus the same way as he or she writes about the funeral of a child abduction victim, or about the Governor's State of the State address. An obvious case: it takes about forty seconds for a bugler to play "Taps". A voicer about a Veterans Day ceremony can be done over the music, with no further editing necessary. Sounds of chanting will enhance a story about a demonstration. Wrangling voices might well underlay a wrap about a hearing on a tax bill.

I'm always impressed when a reporter uses sound so effectively that hardly any copy is needed. This works best when little new information has to be presented. Example:

Chanting crowd:	"They say cut back, we say fight back!"
Reporter, over chanting:	Members of the Human Services Coalition say state budget cuts will leave many poor people unable to feed their children this winter. Elmer Fudd of the South End Family Center warned of the consequences:
Actuality:	"It gets to be a choice of heating or eating. And a civilized society should never force people to make that choice."
Chanting crowd:	"Food before tax cuts! Food before tax cuts!"

(Reporter signs off over chanting)

In two sentences and three actualities, the listener gets a better sense of the demonstration than if the reporter had voiced more copy but used only one cut.

Even silence can be an enhancement, if you do a piece about a newspaper strike from the pressroom of a shut-down newspaper, noting that it is normally impossible to carry on a conversation there, then pausing to let the absence of sound sink in. I recall doing a story about high public employee absenteeism on Fridays by recording it in an empty corridor, turning the mic away from me a bit to pick up the echo. If a story is of a frivolous nature, frivolous sound may be more appropriate than hunting up a spokesperson and dutifully asking a string of questions. Thus, when a children's zoo is set up for the week at a shopping mall, whom better to interview than a vociferous lamb?

Because the anchor introduces the wrap with one lead, and the reporter has a lead of his or her own, there is some stylistic wiggle-room. The anchor can use an evocative lead, such as "Hot tempers at City Hall. Mary Moe reports on a tax-hike hearing:", while the reporter begins with a conventional fact-intensive lead. Being a reporter myself, I like to write a hard lead for the anchor, and start off with something that gives the listener a feel for the story. Here are two examples:

> "Be thankful if you ride MBTA commuter boats—that's the only part of the transit system that would *not* be affected by the fare hikes proposed today."
>
> "Corey Grant was just a kid—a big, strapping football player—but a kid, and he died for reasons not of his own making."

A caveat about some of the more highly-produced forms of wraps discussed here: it takes time to do the job right, in or out of the station. It will almost certainly take several takes to achieve optimum timing and sound levels. Slap-dash production will negate your good intentions. In some cases, a quick voicer or two from the field will buy some time to return to the station and put together a fairly elaborate wrap in the production studio.

Further, not all stories are suited to this kind of treatment. Overdoing it could become a cliche. But some of the techniques outlined here are commonplace in television, and are used to good advantage on such longer-form radio as NPR's "All Things Considered" and AP Radio's "Special Assignment."

Keep these suggestions in mind, and you'll probably come up with more varied and appropriate ways to work actuality into your wraps than the ones included here. You may also wish to order RTNDA's "Sound Ideas" cassette, to learn how other reporters have made creative use of sound.

CHAPTER 7

ROSRs and Going Live

A ROSR Is a ROSR

While most reporting from the field consists of wraps and voicers, the ROSR belongs in every radio reporter's repertoire. The term ROSR, pronounced to rhyme with "bulldozer", stands for "Radio On-Scene Report," and, to my understanding, originated at ABC Radio. It describes an ad-libbed (occasionally scripted) voice piece, recorded as an event is taking place.

When is a ROSR appropriate? An unusually dramatic example came on March 21, 1981, when a Ku Klux Klan rally in Meriden, Connecticut, led to a confrontation with rock-throwing opponents and a belated appearance by State Police. Reporter Bob Michaels, then of WPOP (AM), Hartford, described the melee directly onto tape from the middle of it all. The resulting piece, with the sounds of battle clearly in the background, was riveting, and outstanding radio. (A transcript of this ROSR is found in Appendix Four.)

Examples from my own experience include a champagne-drenched account of the Boston Celtics plowing through an ecstatic crowd on their return from winning an NBA championship, descriptions of the annual Fourth of July concerts on the Charles River Esplanade as the Boston Pops plays the "1812 Overture," and a report on the end of a newspaper strike from the pressroom as the presses are restarted.

The value of a ROSR is the vividness of its communication. Radio is sometimes called the "theater of the mind," because the listener's imagination comes into play. Sure, you could just record the raw sound for use as a bed, and voice the piece in the comfort of a production studio. But your delivery would never sound the same as if you had done the piece in the midst of the event. Your breathlessness, your shouting over the background, even your groping for words all convey information to the listener. No studio wrap can compare with something like, "Here come the National Guardsmen, marching around the corner. And standing behind the barricades on the sidewalk just across from me, there must be at least two hundred demonstrators. It may sound like more than that, because every one of them is angry, and shouting at the Guardsmen." (The example is imaginary, based on no particular event.)

Here are some tips for doing ROSRs, based on sometimes painful experience:

1. Give thought to where you are in relation to the event. If you are too close to hostilities, you could be in physical danger from participants (including police) or from unsympathetic bystanders. Standing too close to hostile participants could cause your piece to be ruined by obscenities. If you are too close to music, your voice could be drowned out. And if you are too far away, the sound may not be very noticeable. Check your recording level; the ambient noise is likely to be much higher than you expected. Stop from time to time to listen to some of your tape on playback. Listen for overmodulation, ambient noise overriding your narration, or signs that your batteries are failing from constant use.

2. Make sure that, in all the excitement, your microphone doesn't become unplugged from the recorder. That has happened to me twice, and in each case I didn't realize it until too late to do the piece over. A short mic cord isn't as likely to get snagged as a longer cord. Wearing an earphone which is

plugged into your recorder's output jack will help spot some (but not all) problems.

3. Make sure that you have the basic factual background before you start recording. Try to hit the basics plus color in each piece, but don't feel you have to tell the entire saga each time. The amount of leeway will vary with the story. Sometimes fifteen seconds from your account, used as an actuality without a signoff, can be even more effective than a thirty- or forty-second piece. And the fifteen-second bite can more easily be accommodated in short newscasts, or by stations that don't normally use voicers or wraps.

4. Plan on doing more pieces than you think you will need. In playing back the pieces later, you may find more little (or even big) flubs than you realized you committed. If you realize as you are recording that you've made a mistake, it's best to start over, rather than pick up after the mistake, since a splice may be noticeable if the background sound has changed. You may need to record a dozen or more ROSRs, to wind up with two real "keepers." Some reporters suggest just keeping up a running commentary into your mic, pausing for a signoff every so often, or when it seems that you've managed several coherent sentences in a row.

5. Don't commit yourself entirely to ROSRs. They are best used as a supplement to voicers and wraps, and may not be appropriate at all for many stories. When covering an event whose nature makes ROSRs appropriate, be sure to record enough raw sound to allow you to do studio voicers, just in case you discover later that you included a factual error in your ROSRs serious enough to warrant killing them all.

6. Observe all the usual precautions against showing personal feeling for or against participants. (Exception: I make it a point to sound enthusiastic during something like a Fourth of July concert.)

If you already have experience with ROSRs, you're probably well aware of their potential for effective reporting, and for frustration and disappointment when one doesn't work. (But since they're on tape, the audience never hears the losers.)

It doesn't take a Ku Klux Klan klash for you to get your feet wet. Simple events, such as parades and football rallies, are good for starters. As you become more sure of yourself, apply the technique to more challenging assignments. With luck, you'll be spared the really nasty stuff . . . but don't count on it. Be ready.

On-Scene Voicers

A close cousin to the ROSR is the scripted voicer recorded on location over ambient sound. A voicer about plans to reconstruct a freeway interchange might be written at the station, then read onto tape at the scene over the sound of passing cars and trucks, using phrases such as "all this traffic" or "the rusted-out steel column I'm standing next to." The location is then included in the reporter's signoff. The story must, of course, embody readily identifiable sound. Nothing would be gained by standing next to a courthouse talking about appointing more judges.

Care should be taken to make sure that sounds which detract from the story are not heard. A story about a peaceful picket line would confuse the listener if the siren of a passing ambulance were heard on the tape.

Why go to the trouble of recording a voicer on-scene? Why not just record sound on scene and use it as a bed for a studio read? Try it both ways. The answer will be self-evident.

Reporting Live

Most jock shows are done live, from the controlled environment of the studio. Ditto most newscasts. But most reporting from the field is done onto tape, for a variety of reasons. These may include the tenuous line of communications with the station, the reporter's desire to have some control over the finished product, and the inadvisability of waiting til air time to feed.

For equally good reasons, however, it may be advisable or necessary to "go live." At such times, the reporter is faced with the need to do a credible and polished report under less than ideal circumstances. Foresight and flexibility are needed.

First comes the problem of how to get the live report on the air. If you are in a fully-equipped news car, within radio or cellular phone range of the station, you've got it made: write your script in your notebook, turn the car radio on for air cue (but low enough to avoid feedback), drape your notebook over the steering wheel, and have at it. But if you are on foot (as at a fire far from where you're parked) or on a borrowed phone in a strange location (pay phone in a drug store, office phone next to someone's news conference), it usually isn't so easy.

First, you'll need air cue. If you carry a tiny radio in your bag, you're set, unless you're deep in the bowels of a large building, or beyond your station's transmitter range. If you don't have a radio, and are working with a walkie-talkie, have the station feed "reverse cue", which is a brief transmission by them, with their mic held next to a monitor speaker, of the intro to your report, ending just as you are to key your mike and begin reporting. If you're on a telephone (including a cellular phone), the station will have to make sure that program is fed on the line, right up to the exact moment you are to speak. Most if not all hybrid telephone interfaces meet this requirement.

Sometimes your cue doesn't come through. Needless to say, if you hear no cue at all, there's nothing you can do but sympathize with the poor announcer who's saying, "Let's go live now, to Jane Reporter, on the scene. Jane? Jane? Well, we'll try to bring you that report in a moment." But if you get partial cue, such as a cessation of reverse feed while the announcer is just beginning the intro, or if you're at a noisy location and can't hear the cue clearly, what do you do? If you are only slightly uncertain as to what is happening, you might key the mic for a couple of seconds, to provide some background noise, then after enough pause to avoid stepping on the intro (you hope,) say something like, "Well, it's pretty noisy here, but I think we're on the air now . . ." That shares with the audience your uncertainty, but in a positive way, so as to explain any glitches in beginning the report. (If there is any chance that you're on, do *not* say, "Am I on? Can someone tell me if I'm on?", because if you are, you sound like a dummy to the audience. And under no circumstances use profanity, because that's precisely the time when you *will* be on, loud and clear.)

If there is substantial uncertainty as to what is happening, you might choose to say nothing, figuring that silence is better than confusion. Having tried both, I incline toward the first approach described above. My reasoning is that the audience is more likely to sympathize with a reporter who's making an evident effort to overcome some sort of problems, than to put up with repeated missed connections.

Once on the air, what do you say? Obviously, if you've had time to write your story, the question is moot. But live reports are often done with little notice, and you may be in the midst of a developing situation. Ad libbing is necessary, but it's a minefield. Here are some suggestions:

1. Jot down a few pertinent details in advance, such as names, numbers and the like. If you don't, and hit a mental block partway through, you sound bad and feel worse.

2. Don't try to "write the story in your head", because you may then forget what you "wrote" and start to flounder. Just review the facts, then clear your mind and spontaneously tell the story.

3. Keep your eyes open for word-pictures. At the scene of an event, absorb all you can before going to do your report. You may see some action that would capture in human terms just what your overall report is about.

4. Don't tell all you know. Unless the event is so important as to merit continuous coverage, hit the major points and get off. I recall with chagrin a Saturday many years ago, when I emerged from a reasonably important news conference, and determined to share my full understanding with the listener. On Monday, my boss silently handed me a cartridge with the report. I listened. It ran three minutes-plus, and rambled on and on. He didn't need to chew me out.

5. Don't try to be Edward R. Murrow. Murrow could ad-lib like Hemingway could write. You and I are human. Just talk, in plain English. Every house fire is a disaster for the people who live there. There's no need to make it sound like the fall of Saigon. At the same time, avoid jargon or descriptions that sound callous.

CHAPTER 8

Filing from the Field

While most reporting takes place outside the station—because that is where news happens—a large proportion of the production is done back at the studio. Filing from the field is often inconvenient. And in the case of very small news operations, it may be impossible, because no one is in the newsroom to take in the piece. But filing from the field is frequently desirable or necessary. In this chapter, we consider the "whether" and the "how" of filing from the field.

Time, Place and Sound

One of the judgement calls we face on a daily basis is whether to file our stories from out where they happen, or return to the studio to take advantage of the production facilities available. The choice goes to the heart of the dual nature of radio news.

To begin, radio is an audio medium. Technical advances have improved studio sound tremendously, to the point where what was state-of-the-art twenty years ago is barely acceptable today. This applies primarily to music programming, but shows up in the better commercials as well. Since news is part of the station's product, one might expect news production to aspire to those same higher audio standards.

But news is a different kind of programming. It deals with things that happen out in the world, not in the studio. Reporting the news implies going to where things happen. If live reports from the field convey a sense of immediacy, believability and excitement, it must follow that reports recorded for later broadcast would benefit from that same sound.

There is no single answer to the question of which is the "better" way to file stories for later broadcast. Decisions will hinge on the factors involved in each story, on the time of day and, not least, the station's own philosophy.

First, why do reports from the field sound different from studio broadcasts? Easy: there's a hundred thousand dollars worth of equipment in the station. The reporter in the field carries minimum equipment, and has a less than ideal means of transmitting material to the station. Seldom does news happen at the end of an 8 kHz equalized phone line. The report from the scene reaches the station by two-way radio, cellular phone or stationary phone. The poor audio quality of field reporting is the result of compromises made in the name of timeliness.

Since timeliness is not a factor in many pieces recorded for later broadcast, why accept the compromises? Why put up with the discomfort of writing in one's notebook, cueing tape on a tiny recorder, and filing from an ice-cold (or sweltering) news car? In a word, perception. The listener has been conditioned to recognize the poor audio quality as an intrinsic part of live, on-the-spot reporting. If follow-up wraps have that same sound, they are perceived as being on-the-spot, hence credible. So we do something that is cumbersome and which degrades the audio quality of the station's broadcast not because we must, but because we want that on-the-spot sound—in effect, for "show biz" considerations. (This, of course, does not apply to those reports filed from the field because there isn't time to get back to the station, or because the reporter must soon move on to another story.)

Here is where station philosophy comes in. If a station, typically FM, stresses high quality sound and state-of-the-art music reproduction on CD or DAT, it may not want to admit any degraded audio elements into its programming. Such a station may not cultivate a strong spot news image anyway, and so might tend to prefer reports produced in the studio, perhaps with multiple actualities and an overlay of ambient sound.

If, however, the station has built a strong news reputation, it wants to do all it can to reinforce that image. Its listeners may be more interested in getting the story than basking in flawless audio. The tendency will be to want pieces filed from the field. Such a station may be able to enjoy improved audio on some stories if it is willing to pay for 8 kHz lines to such places as City Hall or the State House, or for such high-quality means of transmission as a Marti RPU unit or a two-line frequency extender.

Still to be addressed, however, is the nature of the story. The discovery of the body of a murder victim in a wooded area may best be filed from the news car. Any actuality is likely to be pretty stark stuff, which will survive the audio degradation without any loss of impact.

Some stories, however, have strong audio components: a ceremony involving music, a "roast" with lines delivered over laughter, or actualities recorded in a location with a highly-identifiable ambience (a train station, a busy street corner, an echoing corridor.) These stories will benefit from full-fidelity production. If time permits, they should be brought back and produced in the station. If a reporter-on-scene sound is desired, the reporter can write his or her script on the scene and record it onto cassette, complete with an on-location signoff. The elements can then be cut and assembled in the station. The audience gets high-quality sound AND hears ". . . from the Greyhound Bus Station, I'm Jane Doe."

A common-sense consideration remains. Most listeners aren't very knowledgeable about how we work. They may not make much distinction between live and tape. When the listener hears on the 7 am news a taped report from the scene of a fire that was out by 10 pm, does he or she think the reporter a bit of a fool for being someplace where the action was over many hours earlier?

Means of Filing

Throughout this book, various means of filing are alluded to. This section enumerates all means likely to be used. For convenience' sake, we'll categorize them as telephone, broadcast line and radio.

The telephone is virtually ubiquitous. Phones are in public buildings, private offices, neighbors' houses and your own home, and by the side of the road. A polite request will usually gain permission to use just about anyone's telephone. I have filed on borrowed phones from a house next to a fire, a lawyer's office which just happened to be near where I was doing MOS interviews, church offices following memorial services, and even other radio stations. Pay phones vary in audio quality, ambient noise background and degree of privacy. If you're hard up for a pay phone, try a hotel lobby (quiet surroundings, and they're used to strangers) or a hospital (they're always open).

In the past few years, the cellular telephone has come into its own. Cellular phones in news cars, often with tape jacks custom-installed, are gradually replacing two-way radios. Pocket cellulars, or the slightly larger transportable models, are valuable for doing voice reports from outdoor locations or from indoor locations where wired phones are likely to be in short supply. Cellular quality is sometimes less than optimal, especially when the system switches you to a marginal cell. And cellular service is not available in many rural areas.

For all of their ready availability, telephones are frustrating devices when it comes to feeding tape. There is no single way to send good-quality tape over every model. The Voice-Act and alligator clips are close to foolproof, if the phone is an older model whose earphone or mouthpiece cap unscrews. A Gentner Microtel can be used with any telephone whose handset can be disconnected, leaving a modular plug free. Mixer-interface units which have built-in dial pads can substitute for the entire instrument. But some multiple-telephone systems are hostile to feed attachments. I've had unacceptable results trying to use a Microtel with an AT&T Merlin system telephone. When all else fails, hold the mouthpiece down to your recorder's speaker, or use the more-convenient Shure Acoustic Coupler. When using

Figure 1
How News Reports Reach the Radio Station

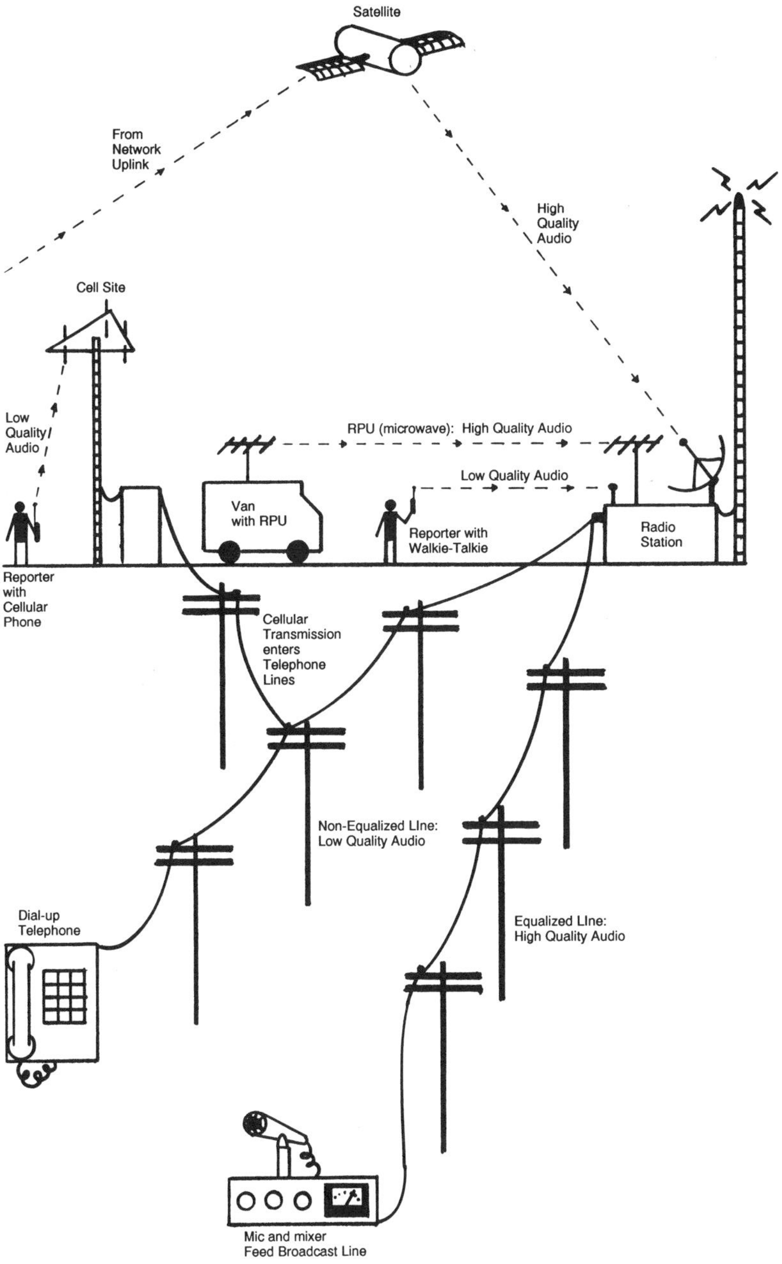

either of the last-mentioned methods, audio distortion is a possibility. If the person on the other end complains that the sound is distorted, turn the volume *down,* even if it means that the person on the other end must turn his or her own volume up for acceptable level.

Two companies, Comrex and Gentner, make frequency extenders which provide improved audio quality, particularly with the models that use two telephone lines simultaneously. But the units are somewhat bulky, require a decoder on the receiving end, and are more costly than other methods listed here. These units are better suited for scheduled special events than for fast-moving spot news converage.

The best method for feeding quality sound is a broadcast loop, installed by the telephone company. Several models of remote mixers are available for use with broadcast lines. A cassette recorder can be used in a pinch. The cost of the line can be high, and the lead time for installation makes this method best suited for permanent settings, such as press rooms. Once a line is in place, that location can serve as a satellite newsroom for feeding a wide variety of material.

A new digital telephone technology is becoming widely available in many parts of the country. The technology takes several forms, and is variously known as ISDN or Switched 56. It provides audio response up to 7.5 kHz, comparable to an

Figure 2
Block diagram of one-line freqency extender.
Courtesy of Comrex Corporation.

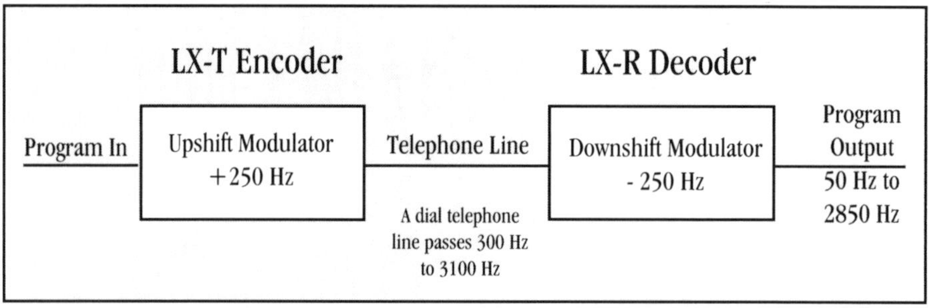

Figure 3
Block diagram of a two-line frequency extender.
Courtesy of Comrex Corporation.

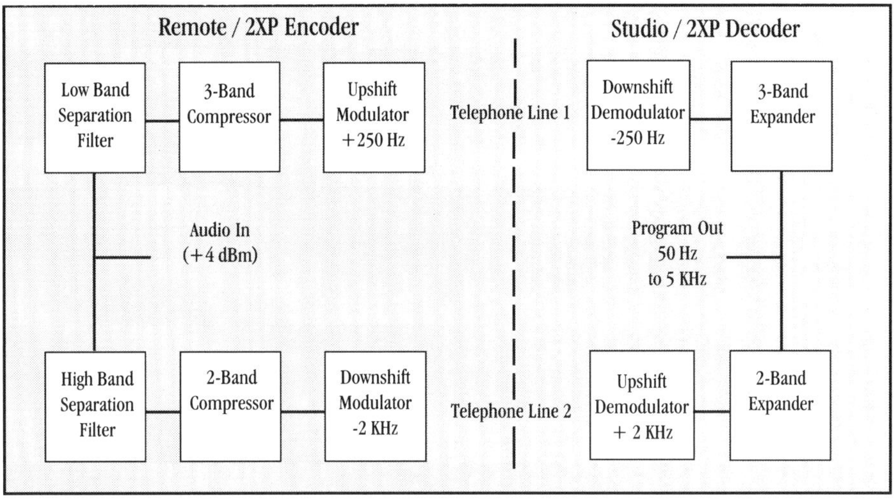

equalized broadcast loop or satellite feed. A Coder-Decoder (Codec) is required at each end, at a cost of about $2000 per unit. Digital costs are such that the service may be an attractive alternative to a broadcast loop for some kinds of applications. The service is not suitable for coverage of spot news. Comrex and Corporate Computer Systems make digital telephone equipment.

If you want to be free of hard-wired connections, and don't have cellular telephone service available (or the boss doesn't want to pay the additional monthly charges,) two-way radios can be useful. Hand-held walkie-talkies have a range of about five miles—less, if tall buildings or rough terrain are present. Higher-power two-way radios mounted in a news car may be good for up to thirty miles, again dependent on terrain or structures. Such radios are permanently mounted, and cannot easily be switched from one car to another. Two-way radios require assigned frequencies, and offer less than ideal audio quality.

Stations wishing high-quality audio in a wireless feed can purchase Remote Pick-Up (RPU) units from Marti or Moseley. Low-powered units about the size of a large paperback book have a useful range of about a mile. Larger units, with directional antennas, have far greater range. For some applications, such as a large outdoor concert, a roving miniature unit can be paired with a high-power repeater in a news car or at a central location. This two-stage arrangement can provide live reports with a high degree of mobility and high audio quality, at a considerable distance from the station. The cost is also high.

Reporting From—Where?

One of the chief benefits of having a reporter on the street is the credibility that those reports gain in the listener's mind because the reporter was there. Unfortunately, we sometimes endanger that credibility by claiming to be places where we are not.

I remember a station in a large city which, many years and a couple of owners ago, used to have its news people sit in the newsroom and telephone stories to the control room, signing off, "Remember, we're on News Patrol." The "News Patrol" tag no doubt led most listeners to think the report came from the field. At least no flat assertion of presence on the scene was made. The practice could have been rationalized as "non-dishonesty." But it wasn't honesty, either.

There is another practice which, while less objectionable, I still find disturbing. Reporters will cover an event at City Hall, the court house or some other location from which filing is relatively inconvenient. Then they go to a location from which filing *is* convenient—in Boston, the State House—file their stories and sign off, "From City Council, I'm Joe Fillintheblank." Well, they WERE there, right? I side with those who contend that that's missing the point. We are where we are, not where we were. If a reporter covers a story at an inconvenient filing location, there are three options beyond criticism:

1. Put up with the inconvenience and file from there anyway.

2. Record the piece on tape at the scene and feed it from a more convenient location, or take the tape back to the station.

3. Feed the piece from the preferred alternate location, signing off with something less specific, such as, "From downtown Metropolis," which preserves the claim of reporting from the field.

Here is how it worked in practice some years ago when I lived and worked in Hartford, and fed stringer pieces to WCBS-AM, New York. One evening, I had a piece to feed, but Tape Ops was busy. I had a dinner engagement thirty miles away. I got into my car and drove for about ten minutes, then pulled over at a pay phone and called in. Since I had crossed the city line (and "from East Hartford" would sound strange,) I had to sign off, "From Connecticut . . ." Is that just being picky? The reader may judge for himself.

More recently, I covered a story in Brattleboro, Vermont, for ABC News. There was no convenient filing location of which I was aware, and the story was not scheduled to air until the following morning. I wrote and recorded the wrap copy while sitting in my car, onto the same cassette which held my interview. I then drove to my home on the edge of Boston, assembled the wrap on equipment in my home, and fed the completed product to New York by telephone.

Other kinds of deceptions sneak (or even boldly march) onto the air. The book *How to Sell Radio Advertising,* by Si Willing (TAB Books, 1977) reproduces the station policy book circulated by a medium market station in Texas. The policy book specified that newsmen were to routinely insert "tells KSEL" or "KSEL reporters on the scene say" into wire stories. That station was not alone. I recall a station in Fort Wayne, Indiana, that used to do the same with wire copy. One may hope that both have long since revised their practices.

Sound from audio services sometimes gets the same treatment: "The WXXX microphone was on hand as President Bush said . . ." The rationalization is usually that the station pays for the audio service, so it in effect hires the audio service's microphone. I suspect the argument is persuasive only to the person voicing it. One large New England station created a link with externally-generated actualities by saying, "WTIC hears Prime Minister Thatcher denounce . . .", or whatever. The term "hears" is passive, so made no claim of having done something the station didn't actually do.

If we're in the accuracy business, we should be accurate about telling how we cover the news.

The Desk vs. The Field

A common practice in radio is to speak of "the WXXX news team" (however large or small.) But whenever somebody is inside and somebody else is outside—if only for a few hours—a natural tension develops. At its most basic, the person on the desk has the big picture, but may not know much about a given story, while the person in the field knows the story he or she is working on, but may not have a clear picture of the overall flow of stories. And each is usually in a hurry.

Let's look at two classic situations. In the first, the reporter is out on a story that has some meat to it. It's timely, it's significant, and the reporter wants it played well—top of the newscast, plenty of time to tell it. But it happens to be a day when other significant stories are developing—locally, nationally or both. The editor (or anchor) must juggle stories and trim story lengths to get them all into the newscast.

"Keep it short," commands the desk.

"But this is a complicated story, and I have some great tape," pleads the reporter.

"You'll go third in the package," says the desk.

"Are you kidding?" sputters the reporter. "This should lead!"

In the second situation, the desk is dying for something to put on the air. And the reporter goes to a routine hearing which produces little that seems newsworthy.

"It's a dog," declares the reporter.

"But it's something. Give me a wrap and we'll lead with it," says the desk.

In a variant, the reporter is sent to story "A", likes the story, then gets a call to drop it and go to story "B" instead.

"But this is an important story," groans the reporter.

"I don't care," says the editor. "We can't miss this other story."

Only in a one-person news department will such situations never arise. At least in large operations where the editor is clearly designated as the person who makes the final decision, the reporter knows he or she must yield if the editor is not persuaded by his/her best arguments. Perhaps most painful are disputes between two people who have equal rank. Then stubbornness can take over.

"Well, it's a dumb story and I'm not going to file," the person in the field may declare.

Or the person on the desk may say, "Sorry, but I'm holding your story til third, no matter what you may want."

I used to think that such problems only happened to me, or at my station. Then I got into conversations with people from other stations, and learned that they ran into the same sorts of things. I have concluded that while the people involved can affect their frequency or severity, disagreements such as these are largely built into the system. It's how we sort things out—earnest-to-heated thirty-second exchanges over the phone, since we haven't time for thoughtful, dispassionate debate.

Are we doomed then, to bellowing at each other and suffering through residual hard feelings? I submit that if the parties can remember that they both work for the same station, and that the job of the station is to put out a high-quality product, then the worst of it can be avoided. Each should make it a point to see the other as an ally, whose motives are not in question. The desk may need to explain to the reporter just which pressing stories are keeping the reporter from leading. The reporter may need to consider alternatives, such as keeping the sound from story "A" to be cut up later, while running off to story "B" now. Both need to avoid getting personal. An idea may seem stupid, but the person who had it is not. Whether someone is or is not lazy or inflexible is best left for some other time. If both sides use some restraint and treat each other like professionals, what really matters is whether, at the end of the day, the job got done.

CHAPTER 9

The Real World

Most of us were not too far into our teens before we began to learn that the world around us was a more complex and less friendly place than we as children had believed. (Some of us, regrettably, learned it earlier than that.) Early in one's broadcasting career, a similar dawning of awareness takes place. Disc jockeys are not carefree stars; broadcasting is not fun and games with a paycheck each Friday; and news people are not Les Nessman clones, on their way to a fourth coveted Silver Sow Award.

For radio news people, the real world consists of more than rounding up news stories like stray sheep and reading them over the air to an uncritical public. Other broadcasters may be less likeable than we'd hoped, or (if competitors) more likeable than we'd imagined. Public officials are every bit as human as we ourselves (I remember meeting the ambassador of a major nation to the United States, and discovering that he had a horrendous case of bad breath.) And the public does not always appreciate us, or even like us very much.

Unwelcome truths such as these are not the exclusive province of radio. Every occupation (including spending a huge trust fund) has its drawbacks. Every activity exists foursquare in the real world, and those engaged in it must accommodate that truth.

That said, it is better to do something that gives us satisfaction at least some of the time, than to engage in something we perceive as relentlessly futile. So some people choose to do news on the radio. In between worries about paying the rent, despair over ever having a normal social life, and doubts about whether the junk food and stress are conducive to good health, we often find it stimulating, and occasionally find it fun.

Working from a Press Room

Unless a reporter spends his or her entire career in very small markets, he or she will eventually encounter a press room. It can be a bit of culture shock.

Depending on the size of the city hall, state house, court house or other edifice, a press room can range from an overgrown broom closet to a suite of rooms larger than the radio station. Broadcasters and print reporters may work in the same space, or may be assigned to separate rooms. Furnishings tend to be hand-me-down. But it has one big advantage over the newsroom back at the station: much more news happens close to the press room than to the station. So radio reporters, even those who don't report full time, often find press rooms good places from which to work.

You, the reporter, benefit in several ways. You get news at the same time as the competition. If your schedule allows only a short visit each day, you will at least get such stories before they show up in next morning's paper. If you have a desk assigned to you or your station, you will be able to stash spare batteries, cassettes and notebooks and perhaps even have a dedicated telephone or—Paradise!—a broadcast loop back to the station for studio-quality sound.

Two attitudinal adjustments need to be made at the outset. The room is virtually always called a *press* room, whether its occupants use printing presses or not. Try as you may, you will not get anyone to call it a *transmitter* room. Not even *news* room, because that gets confused with each reporter's home base, or with the place where the chief official's Press Secretary works. If you find yourself working in a space apart from the print press, don't feel discriminated against. We make different noises than they do. Their noises don't fit well with our needs, and vice versa. Just train the local officials and P-R people to make two stops when they have something to drop off.

The second necessary adjustment is that you are isolated from the rest of the WXXX News Team, and surrounded by The Competition. In truth, working in close proximity to people from other news organizations is a great opportunity. If you spend all of your time in the station, you learn only from the other 1.9 people who make up the WXXX News Department. In a press room, you learn by observation from other people. You'll see how your competitors do it, which is often different from, and sometimes better than, the way it's done back home. And since those people *are* the competition, you will feel a subtle pressure to do your best, since you are being overheard as you file your pieces. (Forget the fact that ten thousand people hear your station's newscast. We all know that it's much more intimidating to be aware that someone from Across the Street is listening.)

Since you are working with competitors, you may find it difficult to maintain the same attitude toward them as is held by those who work entirely inside the station: Kill. You will find that those people are human. And you can't help revealing yourself to be human, too. All to the good, say I. Instead of trying to be the first on the air with the auto accident, you compete at doing the best job of making sense out of a confusing but significant news conference . . . or to be the first to discover that the Mayor's new budget is balanced only by cutting money for street lights.

The usual protocol is that reporters co-operate on non-exclusive stories. When word comes of a news conference, you pass it around to the others; you expect the same of them. You take a phone message for a competitor, and get the same courtesy in response. If your batteries go dead, a competitor gives you a dub. Upon occasion, if two events are scheduled at the same time, and some reporters are assigned to go to one and the others to the second, offers of dubs are exchanged. Everybody benefits. Even so, it's not wise for you or your station to make plans with assumptions in mind. All of the aforementioned are voluntary courtesies, and should not be taken for granted. Obviously, if you use your enterprise to set up a one-on-one with someone, that is yours exclusively. A story you learn on your own is similarly not shared. That's why God put pay phones out in the hall.

In the end, each reporter becomes more productive, and is motivated to do better work; and each news organization is better served by the expanded output of its reporter. The rare reporter who takes advantage of what looks like a free ride is spotted, first by the other reporters, and eventually by his or her employer. Those who do a superior job earn the respect of their peers.

Which brings us to the final benefit of working in a press room: you're plugged into the grapevine. You know better than the inside people what's going on around town and in the news business. You find out first about job openings. And when your station is looking to hire somebody, you can pass on valuable suggestions about potential candidates.

Push, But Nicely

We radio types sometimes become victims of our own feelings of inferiority. I recall an example a few years ago, when reporters of all kinds had gathered at a rural roadside, where a murder victim's body had been found. It was late in the afternoon, and both radio and television people had their respective time pressures. The District Attorney—Ronald Pina, of Bristol County, Massachusetts—had only so much information to give out, and everybody wanted access to him.

All would have benefited from an impromptu news conference, with mics taped to a single light stand. But with six o'clock drawing near, reporters from a couple of large TV stations pushed for one-on-one interviews. Pina's press liaison, Jim Martin, asked out loud if one-on-ones were acceptable, and got very little audible disagreement. So the DA did a series of one-on-ones with half a dozen stations from Boston and Providence, and did not get around to a group Q & A with radio reporters until after 6:30 pm.

Had the DA and his spokesman callously played to the power of the visual medium? Not really. Several of the local radio reporters (I was in effect an out-of-town reporter) had failed to speak up, muttering among themselves that no one would have listened to them anyway.

In a conversation several weeks later, spokesman Martin revealed that he was a former radio and television reporter with a soft spot in his heart for radio. Even so, he was bound to serve his boss, District Attorney Pina, by maintaining good relations with all elements of the press. He understood the needs of each segment, and tried to meet those needs as they were expressed. The key is expressing those needs effectively.

Martin's advice was not to hold back, assuming that you will be passed over in favor of someone else: "It's important that they make themselves known." Attributing some self-defeating behavior by radio reporters to youth and a lack of experience, Martin sympathized, "You don't have any self-confidence because you're just starting out, afraid of embarrassing yourself." He urged that radio people not become defensive when they see television people successfully pressing their case: "I think it's important that they don't become antagonized by what they see around them." Martin recalled times early in his own career when he was "in awe of the next step."

If Jim Martin's words encourage you to push when you have needs, good. But he cautioned that there are right and wrong ways to do that: "I don't like the person who comes and tries to impress me with how he's going to do such a hard-hitting investigation. People with that attitude are interested in their own personal agendas." In other words, hold the arrogance; he's already seen plenty.

Martin prized reporters who do their homework: "I get very impatient with people who ask the same questions over again, who don't keep good records and files [and] have a lack of organization." It's also important to do preliminary fact-finding before contacting him. "They should be well prepared when they call me," he said. "They should have the facts. I should be the last person they call."

From my own experience, I would add the following: Make clear that you have a valid reason for asking for whatever you seek. Don't become defensive or assume a bias that may not be there. Don't couch your appeal in personal terms. Phrase your request positively, sounding as if you expect that you will get what you're seeking. Be prepared, however, to do without if your request is denied. Pushing will get you a lot, but it won't get you everything. And stay on good terms with your contact, because you'll probably need something again sometime.

The Out-of-Town Jasper Syndrome

Our business is different from many others, in that it is just about necessary to move from one community to another, to advance one's career. We cannot hire in at a big company as a trainee, then move up to salesman, district manager, sales manager and finally president. Broadcasters generally must start in small markets (perhaps after interning in medium or large markets,) then work our way up, hopping from the station that pays starvation wages to one that pays a couple of thousand more, in hopes of someday landing a job that pays really well. The problem is that we tend to identify with our markets, and refuse to see those who work in larger or smaller markets as equals. I call this the "Out-of-Town-Jasper Syndrome," after the song "Trouble", from Meredith Willson's "The Music Man."

It works this way: an event of broad interest occurs in Midville, a medium market. The reporters from the local stations cover it. But so do reporters from Metropolis and Tinytown. The reporters from Metropolis seem to feel very important, and may act condescendingly toward those from Midville, speaking to them only to get background information. The reporters from Midville may be in awe of the ones from Metropolis, but certainly resent those "out-of-town Jaspers" walking in and throwing their weight around in getting interviews and hogging news conferences. But then the Midville folks do the same number on the ones from Tinytown, looking down their noses at the Tinytowners' youth, inexperience and lack of information about the story.

The solution, of course, is for all to see one another as colleagues—some farther along than others. The reporters from smaller markets won't feel intimidated if they keep in mind that they will probably move up and land more desirable jobs themselves. The ones in the larger markets can keep their heads from getting too big if they remember their own humble beginnings, perhaps as recently as two or three years ago. And the ones who travel to the scene of the story, no matter what their market of origin, will probably find a warmer welcome if they approach the local reporters with some courtesy, and ask for help when it's convenient.

(For what it's worth, the smaller market reporters may comprehend the seeming arrogance of large market reporters—especially those from wire services and networks—if they bear in mind that those reporters have probably learned that a manner of confidence and self-assurance tends to lead to easier access to people and information than one of timidity. However, it can be overdone, and sometimes is.)

A Smidgen of Paranoia Is Not a Bad Thing

It may come as a surprise, but not everyone out there likes us. Nearly every reporter who spends much time on the street comes face to face with hostility. The problem arises when hostility holds the potential for violence.

One of the worst examples involved ABC News reporter Bill Stewart, who was covering guerilla action in Central America in 1979. At one checkpoint, Stewart approached the man in charge to explain his peaceable purpose. The guerillas shot him dead. Terry Anderson of the Associated Press was a hostage in Lebanon for more than six years, held by people who have little use for free inquiry.

The threat of violence against reporters also exists at the local level, and cannot be ignored. Reporter Gene Hartigan was reminded of that fact while at WEEI. He was working a night shift, which generates a lot of stories involving violence. One night, Hartigan rushed to the scene of a shooting. A man had tried to stage a robbery at an apartment where crack was dealt, and was shot and wounded. Hartigan got his information and tape, and retired to the news car to prepare a live report. After a few minutes, he looked up from his notebook and realized that the police had left the scene. There he was in a car bristling with antennas, late at night, in front of a crack house. He made the live report, but only after hastily relocating to a less threatening locale.

It was not the first threatening situation Hartigan has experienced. He has encountered bystanders to crimes who were not only verbally hostile to being interviewed, but actually went out of their way to bump into him, as if to warn him that he was on their turf.

Hartigan, a Vietnam veteran, takes a moderate view of exposing himself to danger. "There's a certain level of intimidation that you have to put up with," he says, "but that has to be tempered with common sense. If it's an area where police would only venture with guns, then it's bad judgement to go in there." Hartigan does not counsel total avoidance of risk, but he does believe in strategic retreat; "The best reaction to a threatening scene is to get out. You can always come back and get the story, if you are alive and uninjured."

Minority neighborhoods are not the only problem areas. Minority reporters may face less danger in such areas than in some white neighborhoods. And differences in race need not be a factor. During the height of Boston's school desegregation turmoil in the middle 1970's, residents of some white neighborhoods strongly opposed the court's busing order, and believed that the news media were unsympathetic to their concerns. Some residents were overtly hostile to reporters, and my unmarked news car collected a number of dents from bottles and cans. I found it wise to hang my cassette recorder inside my jacket and run the mic cord through my sleeve, holding the mic cupped in my hand. This precaution markedly reduced the harassment I encountered on assignments in those neighborhoods.

How can such things be? Don't people know that we're merely seekers after the truth, bearing ill will to no one, aiding the democratic process by spreading information to the populace? Apparently the message hasn't gotten through, or it has and some people don't care. Or they may not want too much of certain kinds of information getting to the public. But in moments of tension, it's not our job to give unbelievers an earnest lesson in journalism.

We should develop a feel for a situation that enables us to distinguish between mere discomfort and outright danger. We may miss the story if we hang back from some locales. But we can also miss it if we're lying in an emergency room.

Too Close to Home

One of the definitions of news is "that which touches people." Usually, it touches others. Sometimes it touches us.

Jack Williams, an anchor at WBZ-TV, Boston, was reminded of that fact one night in 1987. He was handed, on the air, a story about the auto-accident death of the son of his former long-time air partner, Tony Pepper. Needless to say, he was rattled.

I recall an all-night disc jockey friend who suffered an even worse such surprise. He was in the habit of ripping some copy from the news wire each hour, to read at the top of the hour. One night, he found on the wire a story about the murder of his ex-wife a few hours earlier.

Gerri Miller, News Director of WFRM AM/FM, Coudersport, Pennsylvania, writes:

> "The hardest story I've ever had to do occurred on July 31, 1985. The bodies of the parents of our Operations Manager were found at their home, four miles out of town. They had been killed by a jail escapee who was awaiting trial for murder committed a few months earlier. It was a story we had been following closely [since] the escape a week or more before. I had known the couple all my life, and the Ops Manager and I were the morning shift. In fact, he had hired me. He found out five or ten minutes before he was to go on the air, and I found out about twenty

> minutes later. [I] had to go to work [and] do the story, even though I couldn't get a state police confirmation . . . do a sketchy story, though I knew the details. [I] fed the story to at least ten to fifteen other stations who called all day long. It was everything we could do to get the job done."

Few in broadcasting ever go through such things. But it's not because the stories are so unusual. We air stories about accidents and violent crime all the time. It's just that they seldom involve people close to us. But it takes no genius to realize that, if they are jarring to us when they involve people we know, they must be every bit as jarring to any listener when someone *they* know is involved. Police stories are a basic part of the flow of news. But as we take down the names and type up the details, we must bear in mind their impact on someone in the audience. We must stay human.

To conclude this chapter, I offer a recollection from another city. While talking to the desk sergeant at the police station, I learned that a woman who had stopped by earlier in the day to see about a parking ticket had gone in to use the ladies' room, and to her own great surprise, there gave birth to a baby.

After some thought about what purpose airing the story might serve, I took down some details, but made it a point not to ask the woman's name, then wrote it up and aired it. I felt it would help make people aware that the human condition includes things few of us might anticipate.

An hour later, the station's accountant, a man of about sixty, came to the newsroom, obviously agitated. He said the story had to do with someone on his street, and asked if he could take the copy, so that it wouldn't be in our files. Because of the nature of the story, I complied. It wasn't until a couple of days later, when I overheard someone wonder how the man's daughter was feeling, having come down with some sort of ailment, that I understood his concern.

The point is not that it was *his* daughter, but that it was *someone's* daughter. We need to keep such experiences in mind, as we write and broadcast news stories involving human suffering.

CHAPTER 10

The One-Person News Department

Some parts of this book assume that a station has a news staff of at least three or four, and perhaps far more. But the truth is that the one-person news department (perhaps augmented by a part-timer) is far more common. In this chapter, we set aside talk of reporters in the field filing stories with the people at the desk, and get down to the basics of doing it alone.

Several factors complicate things at the start. The one-person news department may well have other duties, such as running the board for an hour or two each day. He or she may feel isolated, without any other newspeople around to share ideas with. And management may not provide very much in the way of facilities.

You could, of course, work a hundred hours a week. Some managers seem to like that idea a lot. But such obvious things as maintaining one's health and a semblance of a personal life argue against it. Or you could go the other direction, put in your eight hours, say "the hell with it", and go home. Retaining one's job and one's self-respect argue against that. So we explore the middle ground.

There is a fine old adage: working hard is not as good as working smart. So let's make each bit of effort yield the most return. Get organized. Obtain 32 file folders and a pair of scissors. Number the first 31 for the days of the month. On the last, write "Next Month." In these, you put everything that points to future stories: news releases, wire stories, hand-written notes, clippings from the paper (hence, the scissors.)

What goes into your future file? Senator Zilch will speak to the Rotary next Tuesday. In it goes. Sam Outlaw will be sentenced for burglary on the 25th. File it. The Bloodmobile schedule. In. The bridge will be closed til the 23rd for repairs. File it for the 16th and do a story on whether they'll be finished in time. The drug lab will take two weeks to test the confiscated materials. File it for ten days from today, then call them. Public comments on the landfill plan are due on the 19th. Tonight's hearing on a new halfway house was postponed til next Tuesday. Guy at the gas station reminded you that it's been almost a year since the big fire at the skunk works. And on and on. Many days, you'll have three or four stories waiting for you when you arrive in the morning.

Some of those stories require research. Useful Rolodexes are not born; they are added to, a card at a time, and edited, a card at a time, twenty seconds each time, saving you minutes with each use. If your predecessor didn't leave you one, start one. You'll feel silly for a while, having a Rolodex with nineteen cards in it. You'll feel a lot better, after you've accumulated a hundred and fifty. Remember, a major benefit of a Rolodex isn't just the number to call, but whom to ask for, and what his or her title is.

Next, to aid in your research, you wangle a few dozen more file folders. They're for continuing stories: the landfill proposal, the layoffs and possible shutdown of the Fenster plant, the Doakes murder investigation. Clippings go in these, dated, key names and words highlighted or underlined. After a couple of months, you'll find yourself using these story folders in conjunction with your future file and phone rounds, and coming up with some real substance. The clippings can get out of order, so I'd suggest you staple them to sheets of paper, then staple the sheets of paper in chronological order, newest on top.

Now that you have some stories, what's the most efficient way to handle them? Some people like to write an entire newscast on one or two or three sheets of paper. That's fine if you value flowing transitions. Better to write one story per sheet, even if there are a couple of related stories. The story slug goes on top. The slug is to help you find the story later. So avoid generic slugs like MEETING or ACCIDENT. MEET/SCHOOLS or AX/WALNUT are more specific. If you follow breaking police and fire news from hour to hour, try AX/PRELIM, AX/UPDATE and AX/FOLLOW to distinguish one from another.

Now spend ten dollars of the company's money on a rubber stamp:

THIS STORY USED

ON __________ AT __________.

As you pull the story from the typewriter, stamp it and write in the date and time. If the story will hold, and you use it again, note each time. At one station, we had a pair of IN and OUT baskets. Stories still current went on top. Dead ones went on the bottom. The afternoon and evening jocks, who read newscasts after I left for the day, would draw on stories in the top basket to augment wire copy. They'd note times used. One jock would even leave a new story or two each night. One of the first things I'd do each morning was scan the stack to see what happened after I left the day before, then staple it and put it into a file drawer for reference. If a caller inquired about a story we ran at two o'clock, it was easy enough to flip through the wad of copy, looking for "2 PM" notations.

Another benefit of this system was that, if I was tied up during much of the hour chasing a story, spinning records or eating lunch, I could scan the stamps to see which still-current stories hadn't been used in a while, and use them as the core of a hastily-assembled newscast. It was an admirable antidote to the old five-minutes-til-airtime-and-I-don't-have-a-newscast-ready blues.

The best way I know to avoid that problem is to work well ahead of time on everything that's not breaking right now.

At the beginning of your shift, write six or eight stories in rapid succession. Some may be state or national stories. You may write multiple versions of a story you know you'll use more than once. These are to be drawn upon as you go along. Then, immediately after finishing a newscast, lay out in probable order most of the stories to be used next, both new and recycled. Then make your phone calls, or go to lunch, or dash off to the news conference. If you come back ten minutes before airtime, you only need to worry about one story, not the whole 'cast. On a quiet day, you may be working on the eleven o'clock newscast at ten minutes before ten. The ten o'clock 'cast is spread out in front of the air mic, ready to go.

This most-of-a-newscast practice can pay a dividend in the one-person news operation. The boss may want the jock to read newscasts after you leave. But the jock doesn't have time to put together a newscast. So in your last ten minutes on duty, you assemble a couple of newscasts, which the jock can easily top off with late wire copy. You may even want to record a minute and a half or two minutes of undated stories, ending with a spot cue. The jock can begin with a timely top from the wire, hand off to you (on cart), and get a bit of a breather before having to read the scores and weather.

Now let's adapt the "topless" newscast to accommodate a breaking story. At 10:45 am, a big fire breaks out at the furniture store. You hand the jock what you have already put together, then head for the fire. At 10:59, you call in on the phone or two-way. At 11:00:00, the jock plays the news sounder. You deliver the standard format open, report the fire, then hand off to the jock to finish the news. A lot more impressive than having the jock open the newscast and call you in for a report, and miles ahead of topping a studio newscast with three lines about there being a fire. Yes, it would be impractical under many circumstances. But if you did it just once, you'd be "stretching the envelope," and impressing the bejabbers out of the boss.

And if you can't run off to the fire? And the fire department is too busy to talk on the phone? Well, it's a good thing you had that meeting with the sales department—the one when you deputized each of them as auxiliary news reporters.

The meeting when you gave them cards with the newsroom phone number, and showed them how to hold those little cassette recorders they use to play spots for clients up to the phone to feed sound of fire engines. The meeting when you told them they didn't have to know how to write a story, just call in and you'd ask questions, and their answers would make dandy actualities. Oh, sure, that meeting.

And if the fire is 25 miles away, but it's still news, because you don't get fires that big very often in your area? Aren't you glad you had a pizza one Sunday with the news director of the station in that town? Now you can call and ask for a feed of a different kind . . . without pepperoni.

As noted earlier, many solo news directors have other duties, such as a daily talk/interview show. This can be a blessing in disguise, as when a public figure visits the studio for the show. After the show, you hold him or her for a couple of minutes for a quick hard-news interview on something coming up shortly, which you may or may not have discussed during the talk show. That quick interview will become cuts on tomorrow morning's newscasts. (But please, don't use excerpts from your Friday morning show on Monday morning newscasts. That's pushing recycling a little hard.)

At one smallish station, we had several clipboards on the wall. One listed all the fatal traffic accidents, with dates and locations. The information was valuable in filling out stories of new fatals: ". . . the second in less than two months . . .", ". . . only three blocks from where . . .", ". . . Allen County's fourth fatal this year . . .", and so on. The other clipboard listed people we knew to be hospitalized in critical or serious condition as the result of fires or accidents. We'd check conditions each day. Sure, if one died, it was a story. But if the victim recovered and was released, we had that story, too . . . and we used it.

To add to the bag of tricks (or survival techniques) available to the one-person news department, I called on people around the country, all of whom wear that hat. Here are some of their responses:

Gerri Miller of WFRM AM/FM, Coudersport, Pennsylvania, relies on a mastery of basics:

> "Know your market well. I grew up here [and] have been a keen observer of its politics and quirks. It is much easier to write something about a subject that you know well than about one with which you are not all that familiar. If you know the ins and outs of the government structure . . . if you listen to people when you socialize (even if that's meeting them in a hurried trip to the supermarket) then it will be easier to write the news."

Miller also relies on a good command of the English language, keeps a thesaurus and dictionary handy, and draws on what she feels is an extremely good memory.

Gordon Govier of WNWC (FM), Madison, Wisconsin, sent a list of suggestions gathered at the solo newshound (what a title for a business card!) workshop at RTNDA's 1991 Convention:

- Do a focus sheet for announcers, so they know top stories, especially if you're not there.
- Use "800" numbers [maintained by government agencies and trade groups] to get news and sports.
- People experiencing disasters can be better reporters than reporters. Talk to them [locating them in the "criss-cross" street directories available in larger markets].
- For big meetings you can't attend, call ahead and make arrangements to cover them by phone.
- Quality is more important than quantity when time is tight. Concentrate on the hot topic of the day.
- Evaluate if sound is worth the effort to go after it. Best sound bites and actualities contain feelings, not facts.

- Don't get tied down to doing newscasts all the time, every hour. Get out into the community.
- Solicit stringers on the air, to call in observations from events.

Govier says his basic approach is pre-editing, attempting the most time-efficent coverage:

> That means evaluating potential news events beforehand and deciding which are most worth coverage . . . It also often means timing my trip home so that I can cover an event on the way home and then filing the stories from the field or home, instead of making a special trip.

Tight budgets are common problems faced by one-person news departments. Jon Kent, of WSYA AM/FM in Montgomery, Alabama, got a good-looking three-foot mic boom by trading a couple of station tee shirts to a machine shop to have threads cut in one end of a length of 5/8 inch diameter metal tubing, and then adding a hand grip from his son's old bike. Jon adds that he scrounges, never throwing anything away.

Ken Courtright of WBTC (AM), Uhrichsville, Ohio, a veteran of the budget battles, points to some small savings that can add up. To save on teletype and typewriter ribbon costs, a ribbon that has been used on only one side can be turned over for new life. After that, the ribbon can be re-inked using a bottle of stamp pad ink and a small saucer. Allow time to wash the ink stains from your hands afterward.

Courtright is another who speaks of the need to decide what is essential, and what can be foregone. Stations which are affiliated with networks, for example, may be better off to drop the wire service and use a portion of that money to hire a part-time person to go after purely local news. And, he notes, while the one-person news department may not be able to generate as much sound as a larger station, the occasional sound that it does manage—such as from City Council meetings—is noticed and appreciated.

The above "scrounge" suggestions remind me that many small stations do not pay for the paper on which they type news copy. Some type on the back sides of news releases; others use spare sheets from fanfold paper used in wire service printers. That same paper, sold in 2500-sheet boxes for use in computer printers, can be found at bargain prices in office superstores. Fifteen dollars will buy enough to keep a typewriter supplied for six months.

Equipping the One-Person Newsroom

The following are essential items:

- Desk with plenty of drawers.
- Heavy-duty typewriter, preferably a nice old manual boat-anchor.
- Typewriter stand.
- File cabinet, preferably four drawers.
- Armless typist's chair, with casters.
- Scanner for police and fire frequencies. Twenty channels will do.
- In/Out baskets or vertical or horizontal organizer.
- Card file, Rolodex or other brand. One of the smaller models is sufficient.
- City/county street map. Large, at eye level.
- Planning calendar, desk or wall model.
- Cartridge recorder, wired to . . .
- Cassette deck, which is wired to . . .
- Telephone, preferably with hybrid interface.
- Bulletin board, clip boards, or similar means of displaying frequently referred to information.
- Large wastebasket.
- Air monitor speaker, with volume control.

- Stapler.
- Clock: large, accurate.

The following items are desirable but not essential:

- PC-based word processor, preferably with software for capturing and editing wire copy.
- Mixer and microphone for recording voicers and wraps without tying up the production studio.
- AM/FM radio with presets, for monitoring other stations.
- Work table.
- Small bookcase, for directories, reference books and storage of reporting gear.
- Wall-mounted state, U.S. and world maps.
- Wall-mounted schedule of wire service and network feeds.
- Window, to monitor the weather.
- Weather gauges: temperature, wind speed and direction, humidity, rainfall.
- Phone books from beyond your local area. Usually available at no charge.
- Cartridge bulk eraser.
- Second chair, for guests.
- Date/time stamp.

CHAPTER 11

Self-Reliance

Reporters sometimes liken themselves to firefighters: ready to go at a moment's notice, able to deal with whatever comes along. We should remember that the analogy has a corollary: we must make sure that we and our equipment are always ready for duty.

Observe all the things that firefighters do to maintain their readiness: drying hoses, cleaning equipment, testing breathing apparatus, keeping slickers and boots at the ready. Then think of all the times you've learned of a news conference or auto accident and just grabbed the ol' cassette deck and mike and headed for the car. The ol' cassette deck usually works, but not always. If it or some other piece of equipment fails, we may swear a lot . . . but may not change our ways.

If radio reporters were as meticulous as firefighters, we'd break down our equipment bags once a week, remove and test all batteries, clean all battery contacts, clean all recorder heads, test all mike cords and connectors, clean the belly-button lint out of the Swiss Army Knife, and assure that our notebooks were no more than half full. We'd re-coil the extension mike cord that we stuffed into the bag after the luncheon the other day, replenish the telephone/parking meter change stash, rewind all cassettes to the beginning (but off the leader) and make sure that the pocket radio we carry for cues for live reports hasn't become de-tuned by being jostled around in the bag. We'd even check to see if the trusty roll of gaffer's tape is getting low. And every few months, we'd make sure that our press credentials and telephone charge cards are current.

That's a lot of work for a reporter who seldom goes to more than one story a day, usually pretty tame indoor stuff. But if you did it, you'd never find yourself having to take actualities from the first five minutes of the news conference because your batteries were dying fast. And you'd never find yourself asking another reporter to let you daisy-chain through a dub cord because you forgot your mike. (At one recent news event, two of the three radio reporters who showed up had forgotten their mikes. The third, however, had both a dub cord and a spare mike.) And if disaster struck, you'd be making your reputation, not excuses.

At the very least, when you know that something complex, such as election night, is coming up, you should go through the full drill, making sure that everything you carry works, and everything you'll need is in your bag. If there's any doubt, pack spares, ranging from batteries to mike cords. And if you can do all this for a scheduled event, it's only a short step to doing it on a periodic basis. No advance notice is given of tornadoes, plane crashes or prison rebellions.

(At one large station, the morning after a number of minor technical screwups marred a primary election night, the boss called in each reporter without warning, and directed him or her to produce each item of normally-carried equipment and actually demonstrate that it worked. Coverage of the general election, two months later, went far more smoothly.)

By the way, you DO take this gear home with you at night, don't you? A well-maintained bag of equipment does no good sitting under a desk at the station if a big fire breaks out at night near your home. That, by the way, is one point on which you can one-up the firefighter: he doesn't drive his American-LaFrance pumper home with him.

The Way Things Work

The following anecdote really happened: a State House radio reporter called one of his client stations in another part of the state with a legislative story. The newsperson at the station asked him, "Does the Legislature include the House and Senate?"

The story illustrates the need of generalist reporters to learn more about the various systems and processes we encounter. As noted in Chapter Two, we begin each day believing that we can handle a wide range of subjects, including but hardly limited to criminal justice, civil law, medicine, economics, urban affairs and agriculture. Plainly, we do not begin our careers knowledgeable on all those topics. In truth, we don't end them that way, either. But knowledge is power, so let's become powerful.

Too often, we go through the day on a very short time-focus. Our attention is on the next hour's newscast. Tomorrow morning is long-range planning. We run up against a topic we don't understand, dodge around it as best we can, and keep going. Why embrace the unfamiliar, we may feel; it just adds to the confusion. Actually, embracing the unfamiliar is the way to dispel confusion.

Let's go to a meeting of City Council. Items come up for a vote, are passed, and are entered into our notebooks. We got the news we came for, right? Not really. Once we know all the members, plus key staff, and what their functions and philosophies are, and once we know the process by which a proposal is made and considered before reaching the final vote, we'll be a lot better equipped to tell the listener how the community is being governed. We'll be able to do prospective stories on items which may come up for a vote, or which have been scuttled before coming up, and why. It doesn't take a great deal of work, just some methodical accumulation of information. An hour with the City Clerk one quiet afternoon may do the job. A similar approach will be productive with the County Commissioners and School Board.

If your city is fairly large, there may be a number of agencies and authorities that do much of the work. A helpful person in the Mayor's office, or in City Council, could guide you through the maze. Take notes, type up a list, so you don't have to ask again. The same goes for state government, which is much larger than your municipal government, and may be many miles away as well. Talk to your State Representative or Senator, or to a citizen watchdog/lobbying group. Many put out guides to state government, listing the various departments, commissions and offices. The best have names and phone numbers of contact people in each place.

When it comes to the law and finance, it's not so easy. Some local or state bar associations have guides for the public or the press. The station's own attorney, or one known to the GM, may help. It's important to know which level of the court system does what, so that when a newsworthy case—criminal or civil—comes up, you'll know what's going on. Each state has its own quirks, so if you move from one state to another, you'll have to spend some time re-learning the system. For advice on finance, consult equivalent knowledgeable people. Not to understand economics in general or things like how companies or municipalities pay their bills jeopardizes your credibility. If you have a local stockbroker who does a daily business report, you may want to cultivate him or her, and ask for some coaching. Don't assume you'll be laughed at. Unless the individual happens to be the oddball exception, it's likely that he or she will welcome an expression of interest in the field in which they work, and feel flattered that you turned to him or her with your questions.

For understanding of agricultural matters, check the county agricultural extension agent, who is most likely employed by the major state university. The local Chamber of Commerce can often give valuable information on the local employment picture: which companies do what and how many people they employ. On how to deal with the local hospital, I'd suggest you call the President/Executive Director of that hospital some quiet day—not just after you and the emergency room have had a fight on the phone. Major government installations in your vicinity—military bases, dams, parks—probably have public affairs officers who would just love to justify their existence by giving you a briefing. (You might even get a feature story out of it.)

In general, keep in mind that systems created by people can be understood by people, and the people who work in them and thus understand them are no smarter than you are. It's mostly a matter of taking some time and reaching out for the information.

Look It Up!

When we hear the phrase "doing research", we may think of spending hours in dusty archives or library stacks—something very few radio types have time for. But there are several kinds of research that can be done in minutes.

You may never have heard of a "municipal bond prospectus", but they are treasure troves of current, accurate information about your community. When a city or town issues bonds to borrow money, it must prepare a document detailing the current fiscal situation, with accurate projections. No speech-writer's puffery here: bond underwriters demand candor. Go to City Hall, most likely to the Treasurer's office, and ask for the most recent bond prospectus. It will probably be free. It will take a while to understand. A friendly City Councillor may help. There are stories in there, and there is information you can trust in the months ahead.

We radio people are often accused of relying too heavily on the newspaper. Frequently, the criticism is justified. But we don't use the newspaper enough to get the facts about things in the past. Your local public library very likely has micro-film copies of the local paper, or a paper from a nearby large city, going back decades. Or it may still keep the actual news-papers, back in the stacks. Find out now, while there's no rush. Then when something comes up that requires you to know about some event or issue of past years, you can buzz over to the library, look up the newspaper for the date in question (or the following day,) and have reasonably accurate information. That beats asking the Sales Manager or some other station greybeard what they remember.

Elections are a problem for radio people, because we tend to stay at jobs for short periods of time. You may have been working in another state (or were still in school) the last time an election for Governor was held. As it happens, information about elections is important to all kinds of people. Many states publish almanacs of election statistics, generally for free distribution. In Massachusetts, it's called Public Document 43, and is updated every couple of years. How did the winning candidate do in your county, or your city, last time? Who was the losing candidate for Attorney General? Was Representative Doakes unopposed last time around? How does your community's registration by party compare with the state average, or another community? Check the Secretary of State's office. That's probably who publishes it, if there is such a document in your state.

Another valuable source of information about your state is the Legislative Manual. Not all states may have them, and the title may vary from state to state. In Massachusetts, it's about four by five inches, and around 500 pages thick. And free. You'll find the U. S. Constitution, the State Constitution, all Amendments, laws relevant to operation of state government, lists of cities and towns, all elected officials, state agencies, organizations, state bird/tree/flower/etc., and much more. Try your local State Rep or Senator; it's faster than calling around to the Speaker of the House, or Legislative Service Bureau, or whoever may publish the book.

Finally, keep a copy of the World Almanac and Book of Facts handy. Buy a new one each year. Sure, the list of the World's Ten Highest Waterfalls doesn't change. But it contains a very concise list of last year's top stories, top stories of each year going back hundreds of years, lists (with dates) of notable disasters, achievements, inventions and more. Hint: on a quiet day, go through and find some past events whose anniversaries are coming up. Thirtieth anniversary of this, tenth anniversary of that. Phone somebody and get some sound; go check those old newspapers; at least take notice of the date as a kicker.

Don't stop there: create your own reference work. Use a card file, computer or what have you to list the top two or three local stories of each day. After a few months of diligent work, you'll find yourself using it. Someday your successor will thank you. Let's hope he or she keeps it current. People seldom complain about having too much information available.

On the Uses of Newspapers

Funny thing about us broadcast types: we dump all over newspapers, calling them fish-wrappers, and boast that we get the news to people faster—then when the morning or afternoon paper shows up in our newsroom, we rewrite every story in sight.

I once worked for a station that was owned by a newspaper. A copy of the afternoon edition was whisked over to the station, and it was assumed that we (all two of us) would rewrite stories from it. But so did everybody else in town. We all justified this by saying that we barely had staff to cover breaking stories, and couldn't cover beats or stories that required extensive digging, as the newspapers could. But not once did we ever say in our stories, "The Fort Wayne News-Sentinel reports that . . .". Horrors! That would be promoting the competition. But we were happy enough to lift (read "steal") stories from them.

Some will excuse the practice, contending that that's the way everybody does it. But there are stations that do credit stories taken from the newspaper. These stations feel that their own news coverage generates respect, and hold that crediting the stories they do take from the newspaper doesn't diminish them in the eyes of the public.

Crediting creates good will among the print people, since their work is acknowledged. Moreover, if the policy is applied firmly, it flags stories that originated in the paper, so as to shame us into keeping newspaper rewrites to a minimum and staying with stories we've generated.

We *do* generate stories, but we sometimes get a little lazy. With a good future file, kept up to date, a substantial number of stories is available each morning from our own resources. Trial dates. Sentencing dates. Deadlines for filing reports, decisions or candidacies. Follow-up meetings on public issues. All can easily be dropped into the future file and retrieved on the appropriate date. If it takes the daily paper to remind us that today is the day when a committee of City Council is to hold a public hearing on a landfill proposal, shame on us.

Our over-dependence on newspapers takes an additional, more insidious form. We abdicate our news judgement to the city editor of the local paper. If it's in the paper, we've got to run the story. If it's at the top of page one, we've got to lead with it. And if it's not in the paper, forget it—it can't be news. What a statement that practice makes about our confidence in ourselves! Newspaper people make arbitrary judgements, just as we do. They scratch their heads over how to play a story, just as we do (or should). And they make silly mistakes, just as we do. And one of our silly mistakes is slavishly following their silly mistakes.

Let us assume that each person on our radio news staff has been in town long enough to know some of the officials and most of the major issues. Let us further assume that we do talk to some of those local officials each day, by phone if not in person. And finally, let us assume that we can write down brief notes, and make sure they get to the appropriate people or folders. Given those assumptions, it's safe to conclude that we are coming up with stories on our own, and we are coming up with material for the future file. We are probably producing enough decent stories (or could with a bit more effort), over and above what comes off the police scanner, that we could program an entire day's newscasts without once looking at a newspaper. Actually doing so might not be wise, because any news organization comes up with stories that some other news organization misses. But if we could psych ourselves into having confidence in our own efforts and in our news judgements, and look on the newspaper strictly as an insurance policy (just as many newspaper city rooms keep radios tuned to stations whose news they trust), we'd probably do newscasts that were just as satisfying to the public as those we do now.

Hardly any member of the public compares what they hear on the air with what they read in the paper and thinks, "Say, that radio station didn't have this story." Unless our news judgement is badly off-base, they tend to take at face value our assertion that a given story is news. Who gets upset when we don't air a story the paper printed? Maybe the boss. Maybe we need to work on the boss. But first, we need to work on ourselves.

CHAPTER 12

Major News Coverage

The bread and butter of every news department is coverage of such mundane events as city council meetings, police activity and business and labor developments. But (to mix metaphors) the icing on the cake is the major story that invites or requires coverage beyond the station's usual commitment.

- A local political figure is elected or appointed to national office.
- A presidential primary is held in your state.
- The high school band is invited to play at a prestigious event in a distant city.
- A gas explosion destroys four houses in one block.
- An environmental disaster requires a mass evacuation.

If your station acquits itself well, it enhances its reputation in the community, leading to greater listenership and advertising growth. If it stumbles, it suffers public scorn.

With a larger staff or a bigger budget, the station could respond as it might like. But you must make do with limited resources—a situation common in markets of all sizes, including the largest. So your response must be prompt, appropriate to the nature of the event, and efficient.

To the extent that time allows, you should consult with your General Manager. A look at the station budget will determine what is available for covering events with some lead time. In the case of a rapidly-developing story, you'll have to trust that you understand station policy, until you can consult—however hastily—with the GM. Should you err on the side of economy? Or should you "go for it," with the understanding that the station will find the money somehow?

There are irreducible minimums. In the case of a breaking story, be quick, be accurate, and keep exaggerations and rumor from getting on the air. Sidebars can wait: in essence, just tell people which streets are closed. In the case of stories with longer lead times, stay current and provide some kind of reports, preferably with actuality or wraps.

There are several levels of response to either type of story. In the case of the fast-breaking story, your first need is likely to be labor. Perhaps you can call in an off-duty newsperson, or a jock or salesperson. With labor lined up, you can go after detailed information and reports from the field. The portion of this chapter dealing with disasters has some useful suggestions.

If the story is not of an emergency nature, and will take place in your community (such as election night, or a walkathon), labor will still be needed, but you'll have the luxury of being able to slide schedules around in advance. Again, non-news personnel may be willing/eager to take part. If the story is to take place at more than one location, you and the Chief Engineer may have to figure out how to do several remote broadcasts simultaneously or in rapid succession. In the case of the walkathon, a cellular phone or Remote Pickup (RPU) transceiver (such as those made by Marti) can give you continuous mobility. Or two remote rigs can be assembled and leapfrogged, one being moved while the other is on the air. Dry runs are essential to making this kind of coverage work, preferably several days before the event, to allow time for any modifications found necessary.

And if you don't have any or all of the gear mentioned above? You may be able to have one reporter use pay phones along the way (scouted out in advance.) Or you may find people in suitably-located businesses or homes, who are willing to call the station or receive calls as needed. An advertiser who likes the station a lot may be happy to have his or her store credited on-air as a reporting point. And if all you have is one reporter and one cassette recorder, but you want frequent updates? Try enlisting someone of high-school age to relay cassettes back to the station every so often.

If the scheduled major event is in a distant city, you may want to consider an overnight trip for in-person coverage. Some stations have trade deals for airfare and hotel accommodations. If not, the cost may still be acceptable, especially if you can plan a series of reports, some live, some on tape a day or two later. Logistics are much like any other story, except that you go to the airport first. You may be able to arrange to use a studio at a friendly station in the distant city. If not, it's amazing what can be done with a couple of cassette recorders and a set of alligator clips over a hotel-room telephone.

If travel to the distant location is out of the question, try contacting someone at the friendly station just mentioned. They may be willing to provide coverage as a courtesy or for a reasonable fee. If the high school band is going to march in the Tournament of Roses parade, arrange for one or more of the chaperones to call in periodically for interviews. If a public official from your area is being sworn in to a high-ranking Federal post, look for actualities on your network or audio service, then do localized studio wraps around them yourself. (If the network or audio service knows you're looking for sound, they may keep your wishes in mind when planning their coverage of the event.)

Presidential Campaign Coverage

Presidential years present a unique opportunity for major coverage. A challenge exists for stations and news reporters to meet some stringent demands and gain some real satisfaction. It is not a challenge for the faint of heart or shallow of pocket.

During a Presidential campaign, reporters tend to fall into two types, and to act as if they are natural enemies: Local Press and Travelling Press. At any given time, there are a lot more people who qualify as local press, but the travelling press tends to get more attention. They are the ones accompanying the candidate, either on the candidate's plane, or on a separate plane (a.k.a. the "zoo plane") or bus. Timothy Crouse (no relation) did the definitive study of the travelling press in his 1973 book, *The Boys on the Bus*. Many who have read that book recall the antics and hi-jinx more clearly than the parts about the long hours and hard work. Reality is the other way around.

It is frequently possible for "local" reporters to join a travelling candidate's media entourage. What is required is the time and persistence to get to the people planning the tour, the ability to move quickly once the opportunity is presented, and a budget that will cover your costs. Should your station wish to put a reporter on the campaign bus/plane, it should have a clear idea in advance of the expenses involved. The campaign pays for almost nothing. It may be necessary to pay air and bus fares and hotel bills in advance. Meals and other expenses are usually paid by reporters as they travel. Toll calls and overtime can mount up. Campaign travel can easily exceed $1,500 a day.

The people back at the station must be ready to take feeds quickly (during brief planeside filing opportunities) and at odd times (especially where different time zones are involved.) This may require schedule changes in the station. The reporter accompanying the candidate must be prepared for some very long hours. A day that begins with the bus pulling away from the hotel at 6:00 am and ends two states away at 11:00 pm is not unusual. It is, as one colleague described it, an exercise in sleep deprivation.

If you travel with a candidate, here are some things I strongly recommend:

1. Pack clothing and personal items in a single bag that can be carried aboard the plane, preferably with a shoulder strap. Do not check luggage: there isn't time.

2. Forget fashion. Select durable, versatile clothing that can take a lot of rumpling.

3. Pick your equipment very carefully, to keep weight down, while permitting you to operate under varying conditions. A small backup cassette recorder is advisable, as is a short boom for your microphone. A fresh notebook, backup batteries, and a set of numbered cassettes with blank labels are essential.

4. Write pieces in transit, to allow feeding during abbreviated stopovers. Edit tape using an earphone, while on the bus or plane.

5. Where possible, record voicers or wraps while on the ground, partly so that you can save feed time by feeding only the successful take, and partly so that you can truthfully tag out with the actual campaign stop, not the filing location. Natural sound behind your voice helps, but may not be all that evident at the other end of a phone line.

6. When you are given a schedule—usually a highly detailed document—first convert key times to the time zone in which your station is located (so as not to miss feed times), then read the entire schedule over the phone to your station, so that they are never in the dark as to what you are doing or where you're doing it.

7. Never condescend to local people, either citizens or news people. First, it's their town, not yours, and second, they probably know things useful to you that they'd gladly share if you deal with them on a friendly, honest basis.

8. Do as much advance research as possible. The World Almanac, road atlasses, newspapers in your public library, and phone calls to news organizations or local officials are all appropriate, depending on the number of stops planned and the amount of preparation time you have.

It is not necessary, of course, to travel *with* the candidate. A reporter in a station or rental car can hit part of a candidate's itinerary, perhaps in your own or an adjacent state. The cost can thus be kept to a moderate level. The station need not put a second mortgage on the transmitter to afford several one- or two-day trips during primary season, and several more during the general election campaign.

If you are local press at a stop on a candidate's itinerary, you can get a head start by talking with the candidate's advance people. Local party officials generally know who they are. Usually, they'll get in touch with you, because they are looking for coverage. Use the contact to learn about the candidate, about other stops on the trip, and about topics covered during stops in the past few days. One of your jobs will be to determine whether what the candidate says is newsworthy, or merely a rehash of a standard speech. A file of wire service stories and newspaper clippings, kept up to date, can be valuable. Follow unedited campaign coverage on C-SPAN to get a good feel for each candidate's "stump speech."

You would be well advised to be in place early when the candidate visits, partly because of security, and partly to get a good working position and a spot on the mult box. The travelling press typically arrives in a pack, with very little setup time. Tempers can flare when too many people are trying to plug into too few spaces. Should you possess an attentuating patch cord, you could win someone's undying gratitude by allowing him or her to "daisy chain" from your earphone output. Don't let yourself feel intimidated by the travelling press. Their grumpiness may well stem more from fatigue than from any feelings of superiority.

Logistics aside, it's a good idea to sit down and plan how your station will cover the campaign from a journalistic standpoint. Draw up standards and policies embracing what will be covered and how you will augment bare-bones anecdotal wire-service coverage with sidebars, in-depth pieces and long-form programs. Before the campaign, talk with your GM, local party officials and your network (if any), to draw up your game plan. You may find yourself departing from it as developments warrant. But it's better to have something to depart from (and return to) than just do things reactively.

There is a book which will help with your formulation of policies and standards. *Election Coverage: Blueprint for Broadcasters* (listed in Appendix 1) was written by Carla B. Johnston, whose background includes having run for Congress.

Disasters

As noted elsewhere, no advance notice is provided of plane crashes, blizzards or other disasters. But that doesn't mean a news operation must face them unprepared. How a station covers a flood or train wreck is determined by things it did weeks or months before the event. Planning can go a long way toward meeting the challenge. And that planning must be done jointly with the General Manager and Chief Engineer. Planning sessions require the discipline to take some time away from daily operations to discuss something which may never happen.

Here are some points to be considered, in preparing for disasters:

Self-discipline. The newsperson who leaves his or her equipment in the station at night, shambles in to work with a hangover, and perennially drives around with less than a quarter-tank of gas is unlikely to be able to respond when the big one goes down.

Personal equipment. Even if the station keeps only one full kit for news coverage, all staffers likely to cover news in an emergency (read: all staffers) should have assigned to them a minimum kit, including an inexpensive cassette recorder, a decent if not superb mic, a notebook, flashlight and alligator clips. Batteries should be checked every couple of months. These kits should be kept either in the staffer's home or car, and must not be used for any personal purposes.

Studio/newsroom preparedness. A battery-operated radio and scanner, flashlights and manual typewriter will come in handy in a power outage, assuming that an emergency generator will power major studio gear. If there is no emergency generator at the studio, a battery-operated mixer will be needed to feed the line to the transmitter (assuming that the transmitter is at a different location,) or you may need to shift operations to the transmitter.

Transmitter preparedness. Yes, I know how small most transmitter buildings are. But there should be a mixer (old production board?), mic, cassette deck, scanner and typewriter on hand . . . on a shelf on the wall, on a card table . . . wherever. Sit on the floor if you have to. All station personnel should know how to get to the transmitter. Several should have keys. Instructions for putting the emergency setup on the air should be posted prominently. A drill once a year would be a good idea. (Daytime AM's: in case of genuine emergencies, such as flood, blizzard or tornado, precedent exists for remaining on the air past signoff. Check with your station attorney. You'll probably be told that all the FCC requires is that it be told in writing as soon as possible afterward what you did and why you did it.)

Disaster plan book. This is a three-ring binder, with sections for each type of disaster likely in your area. The book should contain names and telephone numbers—including home numbers—of key people at police, fire, civil defense, hospitals, utilities, transportation agencies, major employers and other news organizations, plus elected officials and all station staff. Don't forget a source of a backup emergency generator. Frequencies of all relevant radio channels not already monitored should be included. This book should be separate from the day-to-day Rolodex, and updated at least once a year. Copies should be kept in the homes of the General Manager, News Director and Chief Engineer.

Supplies. This may seem trivial if you're just down the road from a Seven-Eleven. But in three feet of snow (or three feet of water,) you'll need supplies of your own. Canned fruit juices and granola bars keep well. Don't count on the station's refrigerator or hot plate working. Many emergency generators are connected only to key equipment.

A Case Study in Major Coverage

In December 1987, WEEI (AM), Boston, which was then an all-news station, undertook ambitious and innovative coverage of the Reagan-Gorbachev Summit Conference in Washington, D.C. John Rodman, who at the time was WEEI's Vice President for News and Programming, had looked at the ratings for the

Oliver North Iran-Contra testimony the previous May and the hearings on the confirmation of Supreme Court Justice-nominee Robert Bork, and felt that there was a ready audience for the right kind of long-form programming. Accordingly, he laid out a week-long series of reports, most of them live, supplementing the coverage of CBS News and other news sources available to the station. To provide these reports, averaging seventeen per day, from 5:30 am until 7:30 pm, Rodman assembled a team of four people who would spend the week in Washington. A technician went down from Boston the first day to set things up, but from then on, the system was in the hands of the "gang of four." The team consisted of News Director Rodman, who served as anchor-interviewer; Executive Editor Annette Bosworth; and reporters Andrea Carneiro and me.

WEEI rented a studio directly across the street from the hotel whose ballroom served as the International Media Center. Some elements of the operation were traditional. We had four Shure M267 mixers: one at the International Media Center, one in the studio for production, one in the studio for air feeds, and a spare. Dial-up phones were installed at the media center and in the studio. A broadcast loop was installed between the media center and the studio. And we had eight cassette recorders.

Less traditional were the heavy use of hand-held cellular phones, extensive production without reel-to-reel or cartridge decks, use of laptop computers for all scripting, and feeds of all material to Boston via fiber-optics and satellite.

Rented cellular phones were used for communicating among us, since we tended to get spread apart. But they were also used to provide live coverage. Some cellular feeds, such as a Sunday rally on the Mall, were direct to Boston for live use on the air. Others, such as the arrival of Mikhail Gorbachev's motorcade at the Soviet Embassy, were to the Washington studio and integrated into programming originating there. The batteries were rated at thirty minutes of active use, so spares were rotated through a charger.

For production, there was a work station with two cassette recorders, a mike and a Shure mixer. With considerable use of pause buttons, some pre-mixing and a quick hand at changing source cassettes, we were able to do some fairly elaborate production. There were times when we would have welcomed a reel-to-reel or cart deck. But we had to travel light. We wound up the week with a half-hour documentary recapitulating the summit, produced entirely on cassette and fed live to air at 6 pm Friday. As the cassette rolled, we were breaking down. We were packed and on the sidewalk with four crates of gear less than thirty minutes after the end of that program.

All this was done without a typewriter in sight. Four Tandy 102's handled all writing. We had a printer for hard copies, but for the most part, we read copy from the eight-line LCD display. The laptops were also used for communicating via modem with the station's Newstar computer system, allowing us to file scripts, file schedule material for the folowing day, read the wires and see what our editors had slotted for the next several news hours. The documentary was written on a laptop by two people taking turns. And it was delivered entirely from the LCD screen.

Perhaps the biggest innovation, though the one that took the least getting used to, was the use of a satellite to send the reports to Boston. We used the same satellite communications company (IDB) which WEEI used for Boston Celtics Network game feeds and network distribution. The rate for 24-hour-a-day access had become competitive with freqency extenders using multiple dial-up telephone lines. All we saw was a standard modular telephone terminal on the wall. The communications company delivered the signal to the station on a standard loop.

Some additonal notes: Much of the gear WEEI already owned. Some items were purchased for the Summit coverage, then immediately put into use in normal station operations on our return. As dependent as we were on cassette decks, we took a lot of cassettes: 200 sixty-minute cassettes, and 100 twenty-minute cassettes, all unbranded cheapies. We used about two hundred, carefully labelling each one so that we could find things comparatively quickly. We took a multi-line Comrex frequency extender as a backup for the satellite feed, but did not need it.

Not many stations will have a need for anything as elaborate as described here. But we got top-quality audio more simply and cheaper than once was possible. And we were able to save hundreds of pounds, or hundreds of dollars in rentals or shipping, by staying with cassette recorders and laptop computers. Even if your station isn't planning to send four people to a week-long event, many of these lessons can be applied to less-extensive out-of-town coverage.

CHAPTER 13

Avoiding the News-Bunny Syndrome

For as long as radio has been around, the medium has accommodated both entertainment and informational elements, usually without conflict. What usually happens is that one stops and the other begins. But when the two run together, the results can be uneven. Add gender differences and the push-the-envelope concept of irreverent humor, and some real problems can arise. Some women find it difficult to maintain their professional credibility, let alone their personal dignity, while "interacting" with some disc jockeys or jock teams.

Two trends, neither particularly new, occasionally collide. The number of women broadcasting news has been growing for more than two decades. The growth of irreverent, comedy-oriented shows such as "morning zoos" is about as old, if we count the 1971 arrival of Don Imus at WNBC (AM), New York, as an arbitrary starting point. A common feature of such shows is direct involvement of the news and sports people as identifiable personalities. Those people are, however, virtually always subordinate to the lead personality or team. For a woman who comes to work to do news, there are both pitfalls and opportunities: the opportunity to show more than one facet of her personality, and the danger that her role will belittle her journalistic efforts and ultimately herself. It is up to station management and the air talent involved to spot those pitfalls and avoid them.

A particularly disturbing example arose early in 1988 on WBZZ-FM, Pittsburgh. Liz Randolph, a journalist with ten years in radio and nearly three years at the station, was fired after walking out on the station's morning show. Although the personalities were later quoted as saying that they are not "shock jocks," their humor was frequently sexual, and not for those overly concerned with matters of taste. Randolph, the station's News Director (and sole newsperson), objected to a remark attributing specific sexual practices to her. Her union, AFTRA, took the dismissal to arbitration and won a substantial award, accompanied by a strong statement by the arbitrator condemning the jokes aired on the program as "lewd, offensive, sophomoric and in bad taste beyond anything an employee should have to be subjected to."

The station, owned by E-Z Communications, of Fairfax, VA, appealed the arbitrator's award. Meanwhile, Randolph found work at WAMO-AM in the Pittsburgh market, and pursued a lawsuit against the station and the disc jockeys, as well as a sexual harassment complaint. Randolph, a Pittsburgh native with a B.S. in Journalism, told interviewers that she "considers herself a reporter", who "works very hard at localizing stories and getting sound."

When contacted early in 1989 for the article on which this chapter is based, WBZZ General Manager Tex Meyer declined to discuss policies or practices because of the pending civil action. In February 1990, a court in Pittsburgh awarded Randolph nearly $700,000 in damages for defamation of character, intentional infliction of emotional distress and invasion of privacy.

The case is a difficult one for the purposes of this chapter. The remarks which precipitated the walkout are so extreme that unsympathetic bystanders may pooh-pooh problems encountered by newswomen elsewhere, saying that they are comparatively minor, next to the Randolph case. In addition, WBZZ continued to enjoy excellent ratings, which may lead some to assert that the behavior is justified by the competitive nature of the radio business.

The Randolph case drew the attention of broadcasters in Pittsburgh and elsewhere. Fred Honsberger, News Director of KDKA-AM, Pittsburgh, commented that if the incident had happened at his station—a Group W outlet—"the announcer would have been canned." Honsberger spoke well of Randolph, observing "she would always try to do some serious news" while at WBZZ, and added, "I give Liz a lot of credit for standing up for her principles." Diane Sutter, then Corporate Vice President and General Manager of Shamrock Broadcasting's WWSW AM/FM, Pittsburgh, said interaction on her station's morning show (on which the newscaster is a woman) must pass the "Wheaties test": if a "bit" would make a listener choke on his/her breakfast, "it shouldn't be done." The criterion is implicitly a tough one, since WWSW aims its oldies programming at a 25–54 audience, presumably easier to offend than that of a rock station like WBZZ.

Holly Wolfe, then a newscaster at WCCS-AM, Homer City (Indiana), PA, took notice of the arbitrator's award in the Randolph case. The message, she said, is that "you can fight City Hall without being murdered." Even so, she admitted to concern that a management may be as unsympathetic as that of WBZZ: "It kind of scares us. You could end up out of a job." Wolfe doubted that a situation as egregious as Randolph's would arise in a small market: "Personally, I don't think a town like Indiana would tolerate it."

None of the above is intended to build a case for putting a brick wall between disc jockeys and newswomen. A number of people interviewed for the 1989 article asserted that interaction is not only possible but often desirable, given suitable safeguards. Linda Sherman, News Director of oldies-formatted WQSR (FM), Baltimore, welcomed the opportunity to interact with her station's morning jock: "I'm a very serious person, who happens to have a hell of a sense of humor. There's no reason why that shouldn't come through in the show. It doesn't come through in the news." Sherman also aired a daily commentary, "A Broad's Eye View", in which she commented on topics both light and serious. Interacting with three men on

WQSR gave Sherman a chance to bring out various aspects of her personality. "I think a lot of stations don't allow their newsperson to be a full-faceted person," she said.

Sherman's view was similar to that held by Susan Darwin, then at WZOU (FM), Boston. Darwin had a brush with the News-Bunny Syndrome earlier, at WBOS (FM), also Boston. There, a program consultant told her he wanted a "sensational, weird kind of news." Darwin recalls telling the consultant "I don't do that", and reports that he backed off. At WZOU, Darwin said she interacted with the "morning zoo" co-hosts, taking part in sports trivia quizzes, and, ending newscasts with kickers, which the jocks were free to comment on. But the newscasts themselves, she said, were done straight.

The tables were turned at WPOC (FM), Baltimore. On that modern-country station, morning drive newscaster Patrick Nason worked with deejay Laurie DeYoung. Nason had no worry about having his role trivialized: News Director Merrie Street said "it's just not our style." Although a sportscaster engaged in some "chit-chat" with DeYoung, Street said, "we're a very straightforward news department." Street was clear about where she believed the responsibility lay: "If there is a demeaning relationship, it has to come from the top."

While this chapter concerns itself with women who work as newscasters, not "sidekicks", there are cases where the roles are difficult to tell apart. Diane Novak of WCCC-FM, Hartford, CT, reported traffic at two stations in that market before teaming up with "Sebastian", a jock known for his "outrageous" (some would say "offensive") humor at WDRC-FM. After Sebastian was fired from WDRC, the two split up, and Novak worked as a sidekick with a deejay at a station in Waterbury, CT. The two were later reunited at WCCC-FM. Novak voiced news on Sebastian's morning drive show, but made no claim to do "heavy-duty" news reporting. "I don't think I would have time to do heavy news plus work as a sidekick," she said.

WWSW's Diane Sutter believed that a happy medium could be found at her station. Anchor Rose Ryan Douglas worked with two male jocks and a male sportscaster (her husband, Tab Douglas) in what Sutter described as "an adult zoo."

"We do things that are cute and irreverent," said Sutter, but Douglas "is more than capable of holding her own." Sutter made clear that Douglas was a newsperson first: "She's a very credible newsperson, who delivers an excellent product, but she can take part in an entertaining morning program."

Interviews conducted for the 1989 article made clear that, where women newscasters interact successfully with male jocks, there are ground rules, policies and even corporate cultures that prevent a newswoman's role from degenerating from air talent to airhead. WWSW's Sutter emphasized leaving nothing to chance. "The station," she said, "should clearly define to on-air talent what its plan, target and goals are." KDKA's Honsberger pointed to the overall policies of Westinghouse Broadcasting, saying of the Liz Randolph case, "Nothing of that sort would have been tolerated. Group W takes news very seriously." Linda Sherman recalled that "when I came to WQSR, management allowed me to define the role." WZOU's Darwin stated, "The ground rules are 'I respect you and you respect me'. On occasion, a guest comedian will take shots at women. But Mike [Addams, one of the morning zoo's co-hosts] warns them that they're in dangerous territory."

Other factors than attempts to be funny can hinder a newswoman's ability to appear credible on the air. Pat Beaudry of WMAS AM/FM, Springfield, MA, recalled that at a previous job in a small Massachusetts community, the male jock with whom she worked "was personally abusive. He would swear at me through the window while I was doing the newscast. It was very unnerving." While little of this behavior was evident on the air, Beaudry noted that the jock would frequently lead up to the news with the 1960's oldie "The Stripper." Beaudry says she took the problem up with the news director, but because "people shied away from confrontation", nothing was done. Although the jock eventually left, Beaudry said, "In retrospect, I should have been more demanding, but I was new and scared."

Pat Carroll, whose recent work has been at WCBS-AM, New York, and WBUR (FM), Boston, told of walking a tightrope when assigned to broadcast morning drive news at WELI (AM), New Haven, CT. The jock, Ron Rohmer, had been at the station for many years, and was a local celebrity. Carroll told of being warned before taking over the shift that Rohmer might be temperamental and resistant to working with a woman. Since there were no guidelines from management, "I followed my instincts. Once he determined that I had a sense of humor and a healthy respect for his position, he relaxed." Carroll in effect created her own guidelines: "He used the brief headline updates ten minutes before the newscast for some banter. I never let him get me involved in commenting directly about the content of a news story, though he took every opportunity to express his opinions." What developed, recalled Carroll, was healthy: "He never tried to make me seem like an airhead. He played off the 'intelligent newswoman' image contrasted with his 'regular guy' persona. He realized I could make him sound more interesting without making me sound silly."

There remains an intangible pitfall for women who interact with disc jockeys: no matter how carefully the line is drawn between newswoman-with-a-sense-of-humor and ball-of-fluff-who-reads-news, some listeners will misconstrue the interaction. Even as opinions vary as to what is funny or in good taste, they will vary as to what is seemly behavior for a journalist. Male journalists who want to express other facets of their personalities may run into the same problem, but I speculate that women may be held to a stricter standard by some listeners, and by some of their fellow journalists.

Responsibilities for Prevention

In drawing some conclusions, I should first state my own inclination to favor interaction which allows a newswoman (or man, for that matter) to emerge as a three-dimensional person. That said, it is clear that avoiding the News-Bunny Syndrome is the responsibility of three parties. First, station management must decide what it wants and does not want on its air, and communicate that information clearly to all who appear on air. If it chooses to air a high-profile program such as a morning zoo, it should acknowledge the greater risk involved, and clearly draw the lines that must not be crossed. Second, women seeking employment as newscasters (and those discussing new assignments at their present stations) have an obligation to find out what is involved. As WWSW's Diane Sutter noted, "For any on-air person, the most important thing is to be clear on what the station's strategic plan is. [There should be] an open discussion with the Program Director on what is expected of them. Then they should decide if that's what they do best." Finally, one might reasonably hope that disc jockeys who work with female newscasters would follow the example of WELI's Ron Rohmer, and exercise some professional restraint.

Is Newscaster/Disc Jockey Interaction Desirable?

In research conducted for a master's thesis, Peter Finch of KBCO AM/FM, Boulder, CO, attempted to measure "the effect of interaction on the credibility and appeal of a newscaster, and on retention of a newscast by listeners." His experiment did not, however, go into the specific question of how a *woman's* credibility may be affected by interaction.

Finch had two professional broadcasters from San Diego record mock newscasts during a rock music show. All three were the same as far as music and news content was concerned. The only variable was the amount of banter preceding the newscast. Finch writes, "In the first recording the disc jockey merely introduced the newscaster (low interaction). In the second recording the jock and the newscaster joked briefly with one another (medium interaction). In the third recording the two joked at length, and the humor was rather crude and risque (high interaction)."

Finch played the recordings for groups of college students, one recording for each group. The results: "Having the newscaster engage in morning zoo-type craziness with the jock had little effect on the newscaster's credibility. On the other hand, a high degree of joking between the two did have a negative impact upon the newscaster's appeal. With regards to listener recall, the highest level of retention was found among those who heard the recording which featured medium-level interaction (some joking). The lowest level of retention was found among those who heard the recording which featured a high level of interaction (lots of joking)."

Finch notes that the study had some weaknesses, including a narrow demographic sampling and a vulnerability to the subjective judgement of what is funny. And both broadcasters heard in his test recordings were male. But two of Finch's conclusions may be pertinent to a consideration of the News-Bunny Syndrome:

> "As long as the newscaster is all business once the newscast begins (no joking around during the 'cast), it appears that he or she may joke around with a jock without credibility being negatively impacted.
>
> "(T)he newscaster was found to be less appealing when he joked at length with the disc jockey. Assuming that an unappealing newscaster could result in listener tune-out (and therefore lower ratings), a Program Director may want to think twice about having his newscaster get heavily involved in on-air zaniness."

CHAPTER 14

Career Development

As a vocation, radio news is a subset of a subset. Broadcasting is a unique amalgam of show business and advertising, while news is supposedly separate from either. Broadcasting tends to attract people who want variety, stimulation and a chance for self-expression. Big egos are common. People drawn to news are much like those drawn to broadcasting in general, but elements of curiosity and idealism are present as well.

Radio news people sometimes speak of their *profession*. The term is a trifle hifalutin. What we do is really more a *craft,* in which our hands stay clean, but our feet get muddy. While outsiders or newcomers may see this as glamorous, those who have been in the business for a while are acutely aware of the low pay, the stress and the brutal hours. Some of the elements which seemed attractive at the outset wear thin. Those who last are the ones who see their work as a *calling*.

There are three common points of entry into radio:

1. A small-town station where each employee does a variety of things, but a high skill level is not expected. Such stations provide a good place in which to experiment and learn, but few experienced co-workers to serve as mentors.

2. A secondary station in a medium or large market, which cannot afford to hire many highly-experienced employees. You get the benefit of working in a metropolitan area, competing with other stations, but must endure the instability that goes with being at a marginal station.

3. A large and successful station in a large market. Such stations have large staffs, with many entry-level jobs available. You work around experienced, successful people and benefit from exposure to their work attitudes. However, it is unlikely that you will be able to work up into an on-air position.

Students may wish to seek internships at both large and small stations: large stations, to observe the ways of those who are successful; small stations, to get hands-on experience. An internship at a large station may qualify you for a job in a small station. An internship at a small station will carry little weight when applying for a job at a large station. Some internships lead to jobs in the same stations, but not often enough that you should bank on it. Most internships in broadcasting are unpaid.

Those unable to arrange internships through formal channels can sometimes latch onto informal internships. In an earlier era, this was called "being a gofer." If you fetch coffee and help the jock who does the all-request show pull records, you may be allowed to rip the wire and edit a newscast for him or her to read. Or you may land a minimum-wage job running the board for the Sunday morning religious programs. Such arrangements are almost exclusively found in small- and marginal medium-market stations. There's no academic credit, but you get a chance to learn the trade.

It is sometimes possible to progress from an entry-level job to one with more responsibility to a position of prominence and high pay, without leaving your home metropolitan area or state. More often, it is necessary to move from one state to another to find a suitable job. It is this "gypsy" way of life that puts some of the greatest strains on a broadcaster's family. A broadcaster contemplating marriage should give serious thought to whether the partner will willingly endure the moves, the strange towns and the interruptions to his or her own career.

Better to choose a different marriage partner—or different line of work—than to undergo a divorce two or three years down the road.

At some point in his or her career, each broadcaster must decide how far they are willing to move for a job, and to what markets. Distance entails cost, and many radio stations do not pay moving costs. If a job falls through or doesn't work out, the broadcaster is left far from home. Not all job openings are in highly desirable places. And some places which are popular vacation destinations are not very liveable for permanent residents. I offer the thought that you are not marrying the market, and may not stay there more than a year or two. If the job presents a substantial growth opportunity, it may be worth living for a while in an area that doesn't excite you. Besides, you might come to like it.

A word of caution: settling in an area which differs greatly from your home will require a lot of work and flexibility. If you grew up in the New York metropolitan area and are offered a job in rural Tennessee (or vice versa), there will be some culture shock, both for you and those you meet in the new community. Be ready to adapt.

It's All One Big High School

In high school, some of the people in your homeroom showed up in English class, others were around you in Chemistry, and still others turned up in Phys Ed. That's the way it is in radio. People you knew in college scatter in various directions. Coworkers at your first job drift off here and there. By the time you reach your fourth or fifth job, you're either working with people you knew before, or with people who have worked with some of those people.

You should do two things with these people. Get along with them, and stay in touch with them. You may find yourself working with (or for) someone you didn't much like at an earlier job. Lingering hostility can poison the new work setting. Staying in touch with people from earlier jobs can make for a long Christmas card list, but it gives you a ready-made network to tap when looking for a job, for information about a story, or for someone to hire. After enough years pass, the network becomes intergenerational. Your kids hire, get stories from or are hired by their kids. This used to be called the Old Boys' Network. In radio today, the network has become unisex.

Paying Dues

In a letter to RTNDA's *Communicator,* a news broadcaster six months out of college told of deciding reluctantly to go into public relations, because radio didn't pay well enough. While I felt sympathy for the writer, I am inclined to think that radio is better off for her departure.

Having said something so callous, I should explain myself. First, it should be evident long before one finishes college that most radio news jobs are not very well paid. No reader of the *Communicator* should ignore the salary surveys published each year by Dr. Vernon Stone. Those surveys are fundamental career planning material for anyone wishing to work in radio (or televison). The fact is that the business is structured like a pyramid, with many low-paying jobs, relatively few adequate-paying jobs, and very few high-paying jobs. Seven years into my career, I was earning less than guys on the county road crew.

The sad fact is that probably two thirds of the radio newspeople in the United States cannot afford to buy a single-family house, unless they have well-paid spouses. The economics of radio are such that this will probably continue to be so. When more and more stations compete for an advertising dollar that does not grow all that quickly, revenues of all stations, even the biggest, are squeezed. Some owners *are* greedy, make no mistake. Some are over-leveraged. Some really don't care about news. But a lot are simply having a hard time making ends meet.

Second, there is a tendency in young broadcasters to think that they will grow faster than they actually do. A person with a year or two of experience is still a beginner. I hear from news directors that one of the problems in finding good people is overcoming unrealistic expectations of career growth. Having interned at a large station does not assure on-air employment there two years later. Skill, judgement, polish and accumulated factual background take years to acquire. It is common for new hires in top-ten markets to have ten years' experience.

Finally, the business is over-populated. I blame that on the perceived glamour that it has undeservedly acquired; on college instructors who are unwilling to tell students the real odds of their achieving a career in broadcast news; and on saps like me, who encourage interns to keep trying. I have no control over the first two factors, and am ambivalent about the third. I find it difficult but necessary to tell the student that he or she faces an uphill climb after graduation: low pay, limited job openings, erratic schedules and frequent relocation.

Add to this whatever limits may exist to the student's talent, intelligence or motivation, and it's clear that there's only a slim chance that the beginning broadcaster will actually be working in broadcasting five years hence. How many people are truly willing to stand in the mud and work Saturday evenings, year after year, for $260 a week?

Perhaps the biggest favor the veteran can do the neophyte would be to rebuff him or her rudely: "Get out of here, kid! You'll never make it. Why don't you go get a real job?" Those whose emotional committment is limited may fall away immediately, rather than spend a couple of years in agony, wondering why things aren't going as they had expected. Those who are in it for the money or glamour are fooling themselves and taking up space needed by those who belong here. The few who have the determination to stay through the hassles may endure and make a lifetime career of broadcast news. But beware: the winnowing-out process never stops. I know a man who left radio news after twenty years and several awards, because he couldn't crack $400 a week.

Being Young Is Only a Misdemeanor

Having painted such an unpromising picture, I owe a word of encouragement to those who, eyes wide open, go forward. Most news people get into the business when they are fairly young: typically between ages 19 and 23. Almost all, unless the offspring of a news person, start out knowing little or nothing about the subject. But most are enthusiastic, and make it a point to learn as much as possible as quickly as possible. Nevertheless, people much older than they are may refuse to take them very seriously.

This is usually unfair. Hardly anyone ever *feels* callow, even though they may be perceived that way by some of their elders. Frequently, the energy and seriousness of purpose brought to the job by a beginner exceeds that of someone with fifteen or twenty years of experience.

There is a sure cure for this problem, a miracle drug called "birthday cake". Eat enough of it, and the condition will go away. There's nothing like a few gray hairs and wrinkles to get co-workers and the public to take you and the things you say more seriously. While waiting for the cure to take effect, be as patient as possible.

Job-Seeking

There are as many techniques for seeking a job in radio news as there are job seekers. Some work better than others. A method well suited to one person's needs may not be well suited to another's. Most job searches require two basic tools: a resume and an audition tape.

Whole books have been written about assembling a "power" resume. Companies will gladly take your money to write a resume which makes you sound like something you may not be, usually without telling any outright fibs. In general, a beginning broadcaster can get by with one page, neatly listing name, address and phone number; educational attainments; work experience; and some references. You are not obligated to include race, age or marital status, but you may wish to include one or another of those facts. Your educational attainments should be described honestly. The information can be checked, and falsely claiming a degree can cost you a job later on.

Work experience need not be in broadcasting, nor need it be paid. A year as a hospital candy-striper says certain positive things about you, as does a part-time job repairing lawnmowers or a summer spent as a camp counsellor. The employer is looking for evidence of serious purpose, reliability and ability to take responsibility. If you do have broadcast experience, list some of the duties involved and major assignments handled.

Some people advise against listing references, suggesting the line, "References on request." Unless you are hard put to come up with someone who can speak well for you, I favor listing references: it makes it easier for the employer to hire you. List adults who have actually observed you in a work setting. A friend of the family who likes you may be able to attest to your good character. List a member of the clergy if you wish, but I question whether it really helps. Best is someone in broadcasting who actually knows you, and can tell the employer how you function in a broadcast setting. A faculty advisor can substitute if you have no broadcast refences.

Whatever you do in the way of a resume (and accompanying cover letter), make it neat and grammatical. A handwritten resume on three-ring notebook paper is not appropriate for anyone over the age of seventeen. Even if there's no typewriter in your home, you should be able to borrow one. Do not send out a resume with crossovers or strikeouts. A word processor produces the best result; in its absence, type one spotless original, then pay a nickel each to make photocopies at a library or office supply store. And be clean. Ted David, News Director of WNSR Radio in New York City, wrote in a February 1987 article in the *Communicator,* "Why did I receive no fewer than five applications that actually contained food stains on them and in one case literally contained a piece of a string bean?"

The Audition Tape

The purpose of an audition tape is to allow an employer to hear you doing work comparable to what he or she wants done. If you are seeking a news job, don't send a tape of a jock show which just happens to include a newscast. The person doing the hiring may be listening to dozens of tapes in one session. Your goal is not to be thrown into the "B" (not a chance) stack, but to make it into the "A" (good prospect) stack.

In my opinion, a news audition tape (usually a cassette, unless open reel is specified) should be no longer than fifteen minutes. Ninety percent of the decison as to which stack you will wind up in is made in the first thirty seconds. So start with the very best thing you do: a great (short) newscast, a polished production wrap, or a confident-sounding ROSR. Then demonstrate versatility. If you began with a newscast, include some reporting samples; if you led with a wrap, follow with a newscast. Make sure that there's a balance between hard news and lighter material. Women may wish to include some sports in the newscast, to combat any lingering feeling that "women can't do sports." If your voice is less than superb (common among young broadcasters), I'd caution against allowing a voice that's noticeably better than yours to appear on the tape. And spare the poor employer that half-hour documentary that you're so proud of, unless you know that the job involves some long-form programming. Auditions intended for small markets might end with a commercial or two—they're part of the job. If you have additional material that you think shows you to good advantage, note its availability in your letter. First, get into the "A" stack.

By the way, do NOT send out the only copy you have of any tape. Make a master copy of the assembled audition, then dub it onto as many cheapie cassettes as you think you will need or can afford. Listen to each dub, to make sure it contains a clean copy. Label each cassette neatly, including your telephone number. And unless you feel some need to enlarge the station's stock of work cassettes, include a stamped, self-addressed envelope for the cassette's return. (You still may not get it back, but with a SASE, at least you stand a chance.)

Prospecting for a Job

The simplest way to prospect for a job is to drive around and drop off a resume at every radio station you can find. You may stumble onto one with an opening, or an opening may develop soon afterward. But unless you wanted an excuse to go for a drive, it wastes time and gasoline.

A job search falls into several categories:

- Scanning classified ads in *Broadcasting* and *Radio and Records* and responding to those that interest you. The RTNDA mails a biweekly list of jobs to its members. There are several commercial services, using "900" numbers or subcription newsletters to list job openings. They are costly, but if you find a job through one, you may consider the cost well worth while. Your college journalism or communications department may maintain a list of jobs available. Some state broadcasters' associations do the same.
- Placing an ad for yourself in either of the publications above, or with one of the services mentioned in the preceding paragraph. Keep it short, don't plead and emphasize how you can meet the employer's needs.
- Tapping your personal grapevine of broadcasters for word of openings, either at their stations or neighboring stations.
- Blanketing stations in a geographic area with cover letters and resumes. Call letters and addresses can be found in the *Broadcasting Yearbook* or directories published by the Standard Rate and Data Service of Skokie, Illinois. This method is much like the drive-around approach, but saves time and gas.
- Sending applications to stations more selectively drawn from the directories mentioned above. You may choose to weed out stations which show program formats grossly incompatible with your interests, or which appear to be too large or too small for you.

- Targeting one or two stations which very much interest you. In this case, you may wish to include the cassette with the cover letter and resume, and to follow up the mailing with one or more telephone calls. If you fall within the range of people the station normally hires, the hiring executive may advise you of the lack of openings, but invite you to stay in touch. If so, check back every three months or so, unless invited to call more often. Don't pass up a job elsewhere, however, just because of such non-specific encouragement.

The Interview

If you are asked to come in for an interview, dress neatly (just a little more formally than the job requires day-to-day), arrive on time, and be ready to take a writing test and do an in-studio audition. Take a good selection of writing samples and some supplemental cassettes (copies, of course), a spare copy of your resume and any correspondence you've had up to that point.

Much has been written about conducting oneself during a job interview. But with the needs of radio news in mind, be the person the hiring executive would want to have out covering news: alert, intelligent, courteous, self-confident, well-informed, and attentive to what he or she says. Be prepared to discuss your news philosophy, and to demonstrate some knowledge of the station's city of license or home state.

If you live in the station's coverage area, you should have listened to it at length in recent days, and demonstrate familiarity with its programming. If you drove into the station's area for the interview, you should have listened carefully during the drive, except for the time when you monitored their competition. The competing station may come up in the interview.

Don't tell the entire story of your life, don't lie, and don't tell the interviewer how you're going to come in and turn the station around (unless they want someone to do just that).

As the interview ends, be sure to repeat your interest in working for the station. On your return home, promptly send a short bread-and-butter letter, thanking the interviewer for taking time to talk to you. You may want to repeat a point which you want kept in mind. Close by expressing your willingness to provide additional materials or return for a further interview if needed.

To one who feels intimidated by this process, I offer this important point: they need you. Radio stations need good employees. The prospect of having to replace an employee who leaves may fill a manager with apprehension. Can he or she find someone who really meets the station's needs? A poor choice can be disastrous. Each resume is opened and each cassette popped into the playback deck with the hope that "this is the one we're looking for."

Unions

(At the outset of this section, let me disclose that I am, as of this writing, Secretary of the New England local of the American Federation of Television and Radio Artists (AFTRA), and that I served for years as an AFTRA shop steward.)

Many of America's largest and finest radio stations have employees who are represented by a union. Many of America's largest and finest radio stations have employees who are not. Most radio news people who are represented by a union are represented by AFTRA. Less common is representation by the National Association of Broadcast Employees and Technicians (NABET), and the International Brotherhood of Electrical Workers (IBEW). Unions and their activities are governed for the most part by federal laws: the National Labor Relations Act and the Taft-Hartley Act. State laws also govern labor unions, and vary from state to state.

A union is limited by law to concerning itself with four broad areas: wages, benefits, working conditions and job security. In pursuing these areas of concern, a union may negotiate with an employer, file grievances against an employer for acts which violate a contract or law, seek findings of unfair labor practices before state or federal labor authorities, or undertake legal action in a court of law. A union cannot force an employer to do anything that is not contained in a contract or prescribed by law. It cannot force an employer to sign a contract. Nor can it tell an employer how to run his business. A union may employ a strike or informational picketing to apply presure and try to win public support, but both actions are regulated by law. The same laws which give rights to unions also give rights to employers. A balance is thus created, but each side typically feels the other side has too much power.

If you are an employee, you should know the following:

- You do not have to belong to a union to get a job at a union station. In some states, you can be required to join a union within thirty days after going to work for a union-represented station. In other states, those with "right-to-work" laws, you cannot be required to join a union, even if one already represents some or most of the employees there.
- Being a union member will not get you a job. Stations hire whom they please.
- Having accepted your dues, a union owes you conscientious representation and a vigorous defense. But it cannot negotiate pay or other terms of employment more favorable than those contained in the basic contract. Nor can it bail you out if you are incompetent, dishonest, insubordinate or habitually intoxicated.
- If you and other station employees desire union representation, a prescribed series of steps must be taken to schedule an election, to recognize the union as the employees' bargaining agent, and to negotiate a contract. Typically, a union will require evidence that a large majority of employees eligible for representation wishes to be

represented. An organizing campaign is costly and time-consuming to the union, and is not undertaken lightly. You should not undertake such a campaign lightly, either. People do get fired at such times, despite laws protecting employees engaged in such activities. Sometimes they stay fired.

- Should an organizing drive succeed, an initial contract may take a long time to negotiate. The employer cannot be expected to give way gracefully. While an initial contract may well embody improvements in pay and working conditions, it is unlikely that those improvements will vault you to parity with employees of much larger stations.
- Once a contract is negotiated, both sides must abide by it. The company may not be free to deny you the vacation you had coming, but it will be under no obligation to give you a day off just because you want a head start on a vacation weekend. By the way, no two station contracts are the same.
- Relations between the station and its union employees are more formalized than at non-union stations. The station retains full power to program what it wants, and to set reasonable standards for acceptable performance. Union matters are funnelled through the shop steward.
- Somebody among the employees must be willing to serve as shop steward. The post is unpaid, does not relieve its holder from performing his or her usual duties (except during negotiations), and requires a combination of assertiveness and diplomacy. Members of the shop, having elected a shop steward, should be supportive.

Having been rather stern in the preceding paragraphs, I arrive at the two principal benefits of a union: the station cannot play employees off against one another, especially as regards wages; and it cannot capriciously fire employees without a means of redress being available to the employee.

In my view, every union contract is *prima facie* evidence of past management ineptitude. A competent, responsive management which respects its employees and works to earn their respect is unlikely to face an organizing drive. The employees have little need of a union under such conditions. A union is a shield, not a sword.

Moving Into a New Market

Okay, you grew up in Minneapolis, you went to college in Missouri, and you've just been hired to be the afternoon radio newsperson in East Diphthong, Nebraska. You've been in Nebraska twice in your life, both times before the age of two. What to do? You need to fit in as well as possible and avoid losing credibility by sounding like an outsider. Learning about a new market requires a methodical approach.

Presumably, you and your rental trailer will roll into town on Sunday night, with your first shift to begin the next day. Your first task will be to get a motel for a few nights, or, if you're really lucky, to find the home of the staff member who has volunteered a spare room or living room sofa until you find an apartment.

Now, unhook that trailer and go for a drive around town. Your purpose is partly to get dinner, but mostly to get a feel for the place. Spot a couple of major street names. Learn which way downtown is. Note in which directions the industrial, high-income and low-income areas are. Learn where the commercially built-up "strip" is, and locate the big shopping mall(s).

Continue this process over the next few days. First thing Monday morning, buy a city street map at a drug or book store, and a county map from the County Engineer's office, which is probably in the county courthouse. Study both maps. Drive the length of major thoroughfares (I'm assuming that your new job is not in New York, Los Angeles, or some other sprawling metropolitan area), to lay eyes on all neighborhoods and see at least some of the major shopping and working areas. Much of this information will come in handy in a day or two, when you search for an apartment.

On your first day in the station, grab someone who has lived in the area for a long time and knows it well. Sit down with a map and have that person pronounce each place and street name. Take note of any that differ from the obvious. Consider the following: Quincy, Massachusetts, is pronounced "kwinzy"; the Municipal Auditorium in Buffalo, New York, is called "The Aud"; Grabill, Indiana, a suburb of Fort Wayne, is pronounced to rhyme with "table"; Southington, Connecticut, is pronounced "SUTH-ing-tun." And so on.

If possible, make a full set of news rounds with an experienced person, so that you don't make your first visits to City Hall, the police and fire stations and other key locations as an unaccompanied stranger. On your own, hunt up the jail, the largest auditorium, the major schools and colleges. If there is a major river, find and cross the bridges. If there is a waterfront, go see what it looks like, so that you know the docks from the park *before* the night of the five-alarm fire.

Find a history of the city or area and read it. If the people are descended from a wagon train of Lithuanian immigrants, you should know it. If the town is proud to be the birthplace of the inventor of the plastic toothpick, be aware of the fact.

Read the local paper front to back. Read the social notes, the high school sports, the letters to the editor—everything. Listen constantly to your station and to other stations in the market or in neighboring towns.

Learn about the local economy. What looks like a farm town may have several major factories. A grubby-looking town may have very low unemployment, or a beautiful one may be in a localized slump. If the area is primarily agricultural, learn which crops are most important and when the planting and harvest times are. Find out where the airport is, and which airlines serve it. Ditto the train and bus stations.

Learn how the local political system works. Does the Mayor actually run things, or is there a City Manager? When do various boards and commissions meet? Are the schools part of the city government, or are they independent districts? Are services such as water, sewer, buses and ambulances run by the city, by separate authorities or by private companies? Which court handles minor criminal cases, which has jurisdiction over felonies, and which hears civil cases? How, in short, do things differ from the way they were in the last place you lived?

A note of caution: It is common for people in each area to feel that their government is more political than any other, that their transit system is worse run than any other, that their weather is more changeable, etc. If you think that they are mistaken, don't argue with them. It probably pleases them to think as they do. They may also be right.

Learn about your station. How long has it been on the air? What is its power? If the studio is separate from the transmitter, where *is* the transmitter? Does the staion have a directional pattern, and if so, in which direction is the signal strongest? Is your station locally owned, or is it part of a group? Has it recently changed format? Is it successful in terms of audience? Among the staff, who handles engineering and maintenance? Who is in charge of sales, copy, traffic and bookkeeping? Meet them and get to know what kind of people they are. Let them size you up. Find out discreetly which secretary, disc jockey or salesperson wields more influence within the station than you might have guessed.

A new hire is usually given about three months to become familiar with the city, the station and the job. If you approach the task in a methodical way, you can shorten that time to as little as a month, and be doing first-rate work that much sooner.

A Little Off the Top, and Take Out My Sleep Gland, Please

Why I'm not dead, after half a dozen years of sign-on news shifts during the 1960s, I cannot say. Certainly there's nothing in my metabolism that wants to be awake before 9 am. I recall that during my early days of evening shifts, I felt profound sympathy for a colleague who actually had to be on the air at (gasp) 8 am. Then I took a job as News Director in a two-person news department. My first 'cast was at six.

Along with learning to love Tang and Instant Breakfast, and getting used to hearing the other end of the all-night deejay shows, I had to adapt to the concept that traffic lights are merely recommendations. Had I actually stopped for the red ones, I'd never have been on time. As it was, my first newscast of the day generally took less time to edit than to deliver. My principal concern was breath control, to conceal from the listener the fact that I had just sprinted across a parking lot and up a long flight of stairs. Then came the morning when the jock, who put us on the air at 5:35 and ripped the wire to get a forecast and some sports scores, turned off the AP machine and snipped the ribbon with scissors. This, he later explained, was to signal that the ribbon was getting light and needed to be replaced.

At the time, I spent most weekends visiting a lady friend two hundred miles away, a four-hour drive. My usual procedure was to leave her city at 11 Sunday night, drive to the station, and take a two-hour nap before my shift. If I felt really sleepy (defined as imagining more than two big trucks bearing down on me per half-hour of driving), I would pull over and sleep for twenty minutes or so. One balmy night, that wasn't enough, so I pulled over again, somewhat farther on, then again. By the time I straggled into the station, the jock had done the six *and* seven o'clock newscasts for me.

At my next job, things got worse. The first live newscast was at 4:55. As a matter of common decency, the two morning news people would alternate, two weeks at a time. Two weeks of doing the 4:55, then two of coming in at seven. Had I been smart, I would have confined my socializing to milkmen and Cub Scouts. Instead, I evolved a practice of living two twelve-hour days: work eight, sleep four, see friends eight, sleep four. Perfect, except that it left no time for driving to work. I remedied this by driving at speeds of up to 80 miles an hour (slowing to 50 for one traffic light), singing scales and reciting tongue-twisters all the way to become reasonably functional. (I do not recommend that you do any of this yourself, at least not at 80 mph). The ritual was completed by ringing the doorbell and waiting impatiently while the engineer shuffled out to let me in. The evening guy was very good about leaving fresh sound with scripts, so a fairly decent-sounding newscast could be created in a couple of minutes.

Less perilous, but more bizarre, was my experience several years earlier, while working for a classical-music FM. I normally worked the late evening board shift, but one time was obligated to do the Saturday sign-on shift as well. My plan was to sack out at the station. But I got to reading and decided to just stay up. By seven or thereabouts, I realized this had been a poor decision, but it was too late. The morning wore on. At eleven, a block of music from records was followed by a five-minute newscast and a transcribed-on-disc show. I awoke with a start at 11:10, expecting dead air. What I found was that the records had been put away; the news copy initialled, stapled and put on the shelf; the transcribed show was on the air; and the log was filled out. I had done it all in my sleep!

APPENDIX 1

Reading List

This list is not intended to be comprehensive. It focuses on books which deal in greater detail with topics covered in this book, and omits books which deal primarily with television.

Barnouw, Erik, *A Tower in Babel,* Oxford University Press, New York, 1966.

Barnouw, Erik, *Mass Communication,* Holt, Rinehart and Winston, New York, 1966.

Barnouw, Erik, *The Golden Web,* Oxford University Press, New York, 1968.

Barrett, Marvin, ed., *The Politics of Broadcasting—Alfred I. duPont-Columbia University Survey of Broadcast Journalism—1971-1972,* Thomas Y. Crowell, New York, 1973.

Bedell Smith, Sally, *In All His Glory—The Life of William S. Paley, The Legendary Tycoon and His Brilliant Circle,* Simon and Schuster, New York, 1990.

Bliss, Edward, Jr., ed., *In Search of Light—The Broadcasts of Edward R. Murrow, 1938-1961,* Alfred A. Knopf, New York, 1967.

Bliss, Edward, Jr., *Now the News—The Story of Broadcast Journalism,* Columbia University Press, New York, 1991.

Bliss, Edward, Jr., and Patterson, John M., *Writing News for Broadcast,* 2nd edition—fully revised, Columbia University Press, New York, 1978.

Block, Mervin, *Rewriting Network News: Wordwatching Tips from 345 Network TV and Radio Scripts,* Bonus Books, Chicago, 1990

Block, Mervin, *Writing Broadcast News—Shorter, Sharper, Stronger,* Bonus Books, Chicago, 1987.

Blume, Dan, *Making it in Radio,* Continental Media Company, Hartford, Connecticut, 1983.

Charnley, Mitchell, *News by Radio,* Macmillan, New York, 1948.

Cooper, Kent, *Barriers Down—The Story of the News Agency Epoch,* Kennikat Press, Port Washington, New York, 1969.

Crouse, Timothy, *The Boys on the Bus—Riding with the Campaign Press Corps,* Random House, New York, 1972.

Fang, Irving E., *Television News, Radio News,* Rada Press, St. Paul, Minnesota, 1972.

Fang, Irving E., *Those Radio Commentators!,* Iowa State University Press, Ames, Iowa, 1977.

Fornatale, Peter, and Mills, Joshua E., *Radio in the Television Age,* Overlook Press, Woodstock, New York, 1980.

Gates, Gary Paul, *Air Time—The Inside Story of CBS News,* Harper and Row, New York, 1978.

Gifford, F., *Tape—A Radio News Handbook,* Hastings House, New York, 1977.

Gordon, George N., and Falk, Irving A., *On the Spot Reporting—Radio Records History,* Julian Messner, New York, 1967.

Gross, Ben, *I Looked & I Listened,* Arlington House, New Rochelle, New York, 1954.

Johnston, Carla B., *Election Coverage—Blueprint for Broadcasters,* Focal Press, Stoneham, Massachusetts, 1991.

Keirstead, Phillip O., *All-News Radio,* TAB Books, Blue Ridge Summit, Pennsylvania, 1980.

Keirstead, Phillip O., *Journalist's Handbook of Live TV-Radio News,* TAB Books, Blue Ridge Sunnit, Pennsylvania, 1976.

Kendrick, Alexander, *Prime Time—The Life of Edward R. Murrow,* Little Brown, Boston 1969.

King, Larry and Yoffe, Emily, *Larry King by Larry King,* Simon and Schuster, New York, 1982.

Lewis, Tom, *Empire of the Air—The Creation of Radio,* Harper-Collins, New York, 1991.

Lyons, Eugene, *David Sarnoff, a Biography,* Harper and Row, New York, 1966.

MacVane, John, *On the Air in World War II,* William B. Morrow, New York, 1979.

O'Donnell, Lewis B., Benoit, Philip, and Hausman, Carl, *Modern Radio Production,* Wentworth Publishing, Belmont, California, 1988.

Oringel, Robert S., *Audio Control Handbook for Radio and Television Broadcasting,* Hastings House, New York, 1983.

Paiva, Bob, *The Program Director's Handbook,* TAB Books, Blue Ridge Summit, Pennsylvania, 1983.

Pearlman, Donn, *Breaking into Broadcasting,* Bonus Books, Inc., Chicago, 1987.

Perry, Dick, *Not Just a Sound—The Story of WLW,* Prentice-Hall, Englewood Cliffs, New Jersey, 1971.

Poindexter, Ray, *Golden Throats and Silver Tongues—The Radio Announcers,* River Road Press, Conway, Arkansas, 1978.

Powers, Ron, *The Newscasters—The News Business as Show Business,* St. Martin's Press, New York, 1977.

Quinlan, Sterling, *Inside ABC—American Broadcasting Company's Rise to Power,* Hastings House, New York, 1979.

Schechter, A. A. and Anthony, Edward, *I Live on Air,* Frederick A. Stokes, New York, 1941.

Siller, Bob, White, Ted and Terkel, Hal, *Television and Radio News,* Macmillan, New York, 1960.

Sklar, Rick, *Rocking America—How the All-Hit Radio Stations Took Over,* St. Martin's Press, New York, 1984.

Slater, Robert, *This . . . Is CBS—A Chronicle of 60 Years,* Prentice-Hall, Englewood Cliffs, New Jersey, 1988.

Sperber, A. M., *Murrow: His Life and Times,* Freundlich Books, New York, 1986.

Stephens, Mitchell, *Broadcast News—Radio Journalism and an Introduction to Television,* Holt Rinehart and Winston, New York, 1980.

White, Paul W., *News On the Air,* Harcourt, Brace, New York, 1947.

White, Ted, Meppen, Adrian J. and Young, Steve, *Broadcast News Writing, Reporting and Production,* MacMillan, New York, 1984.

A P P E N D I X 2

91 Steps to Better Writing

The steps listed here include many cliches and wrong word choices often found in news writing. Any news writer would benefit by having one of the leading books on usage at hand. I used Theodore M. Bernstein's *The Careful Writer,* Athaneum, 1983. Many books on broadcast news writing have appeared over the years. My favorite is Mervin Block's *Writing Broadcast News: Shorter, Sharper, Stronger,* Bonus Books, 1987.

Scan the laundry list that follows, until you spot a couple of your own bad habits. Make a conscious effort to eliminate those bad habits. Then come back for more.

1. *Laundry list*

I wasn't writing about laundry. The word "list" would have sufficed.

2. *Accident scene*

An accident—for most newswriting purposes—is a collision or other mishap involving one or more motor vehicles. An accident scene is the place where it happens. It is the accident, or its aftermath, not the scene of the accident, which is holding up freeway traffic.

3. *Accused/alleged murderer*

"Accused" is an adjective modifying the noun "murderer." You are calling the person a murderer.

4. *Acronyms*

Everybody knows what NATO is. Do all of your listeners know what a UDAG is? When in doubt, give the full phrase in the first reference.

5. *Active voice*

Sentences written in the active voice tend to be shorter and more direct than those written in the passive voice. There are exceptions. But before writing a sentence in the passive voice, ask yourself whether it's really necessary.

6. *Advance warning, advance planning*

Now seriously, is there any other kind? The same goes for "pre-planning."

7. *Amount/number*

"Amount" applies to non-enumerable quantities, "number" to those which can be counted. An amount of money, a number of people.

8. *Another/more*

"Another" means one more of the same kind. In writing of successive but different numbers, say "Ten thousand people filed past the tomb Monday, and eight thousand more yesterday."

9. *Arraignment/bail hearing*

The initial appearance in court by an accused person is usually for the setting of bail. Only later does the accused actually enter a plea, which appearance is called an arraignment.

10. *Attribution of attitude*

Mayor Smith may say that he is angry/disappointed/outraged. But he may just be saying so for effect. We don't know whether Mayor Smith *is* angry. We do know that he *says* he is. Report the known fact.

11. *Back-identification of disaster locations*

The story will benefit, and some listeners will be reassured, if you repeat the location of a calamity near the end of the story.

12. *Bill/law*

A piece of legislation is a bill until it is signed, after which it is a law. The document the governor signs is a bill.

13. *Breakthrough*

In reporting on medical research, it's wise not to use the term unless the researcher does. The same often applies to reporting on criminal investigations.

14. *Bring/take*

"Bring" implies movement toward the speaker. Citizens are not "bringing" unregistered guns to the police station unless the reporter is at that location. I will "take" a sandwich to work tomorrow.

15. *Buff/fan/collector*

"Buff" is a term used by one who does not share an avocation. It sounds patronizing. People who like trains call themselves "railfans." Also, "old car collector", "Civil War historian", "Elvis fan".

16. *Claims credit for*

The terrorist group cannot claim credit for the bombing, because the act does not deserve credit. They claim responsibility.

17. *Compound sentences*

Should be broken up into two simple sentences.

18. *Controversial*

A vague and over-used term. If an issue is in dispute, note the opposing view.

19. *Convince/persuade*

"Convince" implies a high degree of certainty. If I talk you into supporting my plan, I have probably only persuaded you.

20. *Criterion/criteria*

If only one test must be met, it is a "criterion."

21. *Cutesy writing*

Writing which calls attention to itself draws attention away from the story. Avoid most puns, alliterations, rhymes and folksy figures of speech. Creative writing is fine, but "bungled burglary" is not creative.

22. *Dead bodies*

News people seldom write about bodies that are not dead.

23. *Decimate*

Writers seem to think this word has a nice "splat!" sound to it. It means to kill every tenth person. A better choice would be "devastate", "destroy", "obliterate" or just "wipe out."

24. *Dilemma/problem/predicament*

The landfill issue facing city council is a dilemma only if it involves two choices, equally distasteful. If it is merely a thorny problem, find another word. "Predicament" means a difficult situation.

25. *Double negatives*

These are seemingly literate figures of speech, like "not uncommon", "not unheard of", "not unfamiliar with". There is a shorter, more direct way of saying the same thing.

26. *Double passives*

After cutting our teeth on simple passives ("The condemned killer was hanged."), we can move on to such monstrosities as Bernstein's "The runaway horse was attempted to be stopped by the policeman." Or we can write a far simpler sentence in the active voice.

27. *Drugs/narcotics*
All narcotics are drugs, but not all drugs are narcotics. A narcotic drug dulls the senses and induces sleep. Cocaine, LSD and amphetamines should not be called narcotics.

28. *Ellipsis marks in place of conventional punctuation*
What is the following sentence saying? "The Democrats . . . say the Republicans . . . are sure to win the election." (Example adapted from Bernstein.)

29. *Fewer/less*
"Fewer" applies to quantities that can be counted. I have less money, fewer dollars. There is less water in the bucket. The state has fewer employees.

30. *Fire/dismiss/lay off*
"Fire" is seen by purists as slang, but is well established colloquially. However, it has a connotation of dismissal for cause. In cases of reduction of staff, the term "lay off" is preferable.

31. *Firm/company*
A firm is a partnership. The term is not appropriate for a sole proprietorship or corporation. "Company" is simple and broad. "Business" is a good umbrella synonym.

32. *Forms of "to be"*
Omission of "be, am, is, are, was, were" is neither direct nor conversational, and opens the way to listener confusion.

33. *Gearing up for*
As a substitute for "preparing for", this cliche is overdue for retirement.

34. *Gender-dependent second reference*
If the story is about Homer Smith, only the *New York Times* will use the honorific "Mr." on second reference. The rest of us will write "Smith". If the story is about Helen Smith, the procedure should be the same. If the story is about a married

couple named Smith, "Mr." and "Mrs." helps tell the two apart. But be sure they're not brother and sister, or mother and son.

35. *Hijack*

Does not mean to take hostage, particularly when talking about a public official taking an issue hostage as a way of getting his or her way.

36. *Homonyms*

Words with multiple meanings can create problems. Be careful with "pool" (body of water, joint contributions or billiards), "sanction" (approve or enforcement) and "pass" (approve or skip over).

37. *Homophones*

A "cache of drug money" makes sense on paper, but is confusing to the ear. A few others cited by Block are: aides/AIDS, formally/formerly, and raise/raze. Listen as you write.

38. *Hopeful that*

I am hopeful that the rain will let up. I hope the rain will let up. Which is simpler and more direct?

39. *Impact*

This noun, as a synonym for "effect", has been overused and devalued. As a transitive verb, it is bureaucratic jargon.

40. *Implementation*

More bureaucrat-speak. It means "putting into effect" or "carrying out."

41. *Imply/infer*

Frequently confused. "Imply" means to hint or say something indirectly. "Infer" means to deduce or draw a conclusion.

42. *Incident*

Except in diplomacy (in which it means something likely to have grave consequences) "incident" means "occurrence or happening." Its use to describe a serious crime or public disorder injects a note of triviality.

43. *Indicate*

Despite the jargon of bureaucrats, this word does not mean "say" or "tell." It means to point out, or to state something briefly or indirectly.

44. *Indefinitely*

Often used to suggest "beyond the forseeable future." It means "without defined limits." The plant, shut down indefinitely, thus *could* re-open tomorrow morning.

45. *In order to*

Use only if you're being paid by the word. Means "to". The same goes for "on the topic of", "for the purpose of", "in terms of", "in the course of", and "at the present time."

46. *Ironically*

The dictionary says that "ironically" means marked by irony, which is a form of sarcasm or an unexpected result. In use, "ironically" usually suggests a twist of fate. Misused, it indicates a mere quirk of facts.

47. *Is not known*

"Foonman's whereabouts are not known." Well, not by me. Foonman probably knows, as may his wife, lawyer, mother, close friends . . .

48. *Jail/prison*

A jail is a place for comparatively short-term confinement, especially of suspects awaiting trial or those serving time for misdemeanors. A prison is generally reserved for those convicted of felonies.

49. *Kick off*

Like "gear up for", "kick off" is a once-useful figure of speech that became trite long ago.

50. *Libel/slander*

Both terms refer to defamation or causing injury to another's reputation. Libel is accomplished in writing; slander is committed orally. Even so, defamation by broadcast is libel.

51. *Like/as if*

Back in the seventh grade, Miss Smithers told you not to use "like" in place of "as if." Like Miss Smithers, I urge you to obey the rule as if it were written in stone. The preceding sentence illustrates the rule's application: In drawing comparisons, "like" may precede a noun, but "as if" precedes a verb, in this case "were."

52. *Literally*

All too often, "literally" ("the letter of the statement is true") is used as if it meant "in a manner of speaking", which is the exact opposite. The word is hardly ever necessary; why use it at all?

53. *Livid*

Means "ashen . . . deadly pale". If you want to convey "angry", write "angry" or "furious" or "enraged". "Ballistic" was an 80's newsmagazine buzzword.

54. *Loner*

The crutch of the unimaginative reporter assigned to do background on a crime suspect. If he wasn't demonstrably gregarious, the suspect was "a loner". Does that tell us anything germane to the issue?

55. *Major*

An overworked adjective, beloved of people writing promos for late-evening TV newscasts. The more we use it, the less it means.

56. *Meanwhile (used as a transition between stories)*

The president vetoes a bill. Meanwhile, the Queen of England makes an appearance. There is no connection. And the two events probably didn't happen at the same time.

57. *Medium/media*

Radio is a medium. Radio, TV and newspapers are news media. Radio, billboards and matchbook covers are advertising media. The radio station you work for is a news organization. If a member of the public says, "The media is always . . .", we can forgive him or her. If we do it, shame on us.

58. *Near-miss*

The planes nearly missed, eh? Too bad: aluminum shower. A more accurate term is "near collision."

59. *New innovation*

Is there any other kind? The same goes for "old adage".

60. *Not guilty/innocent*

Sit in a courtroom for the rest of your life, and you will never hear a defendant plead innocent, or a jury return a verdict of innocent. The term is "not guilty", which means something less sweeping than "innocent." There is a hoary rationale that the listener may not hear the word "not". So emphasize "not" when you read the copy.

61. *On charges of*

Unless you know that the suspect has been charged with more than one offense, write that he or she is being held "on a charge of" constribulation, or whatever.

62. *Participate*

A fifty-cent word. "Take part" or "attend" only cost a quarter.

63. *People/persons*

Some persons think that "people" sounds vague, or should only be used with large numbers. I asked several persons on the street corner about it, and they laughed at me.

64. *Police and fire department jargon*

Cops have to say things like, "Officers apprehended the suspect and placed him in custody." We don't. The fire chief may tell you, "The structure was fully involved when the first unit arrived, but we had it knocked down within a hour." We are free under the First Ammendment to translate that into English.

65. *Procedural jargon*

Many of the people (sorry . . . persons) we deal with use jargon, and after awhile we come to understand it. But most members of the public don't. Translate.

66. *Pupil/student*

A student is one who studies; a pupil is one who is taught. "Student" is generally applied to people in high school and college. As to junior high, it's your call.

67. *Refute/Rebut/Dispute*

To refute is to prove false by argument or evidence. If Mayor Snerd is accused of mismanagement, he will *attempt* to refute the charge, but unless you are totally won over and willing to be his defender on the air, you should write that he "rebutted" or "disputed" the charge.

68. *Reverend*

Properly, a clergyman should be called "The Reverend Mr. Doe"; but in many quarters, "Reverend Doe" is acceptable. However, never speak of John Doe as "a reverend", as a synonym for "minister" or "clergyman."

69. *Risk/chance*

Some weather forecasters speak of "a risk of showers." "Risk" means "danger or peril." "Chance" is preferable.

70. *Serve out*

A prisoner serves a sentence; a county commissioner serves a term. The word "out" is unnecessary.

71. *Showed no emotion as*

A crutch of courtroom reporters, as if the accused is a soap opera character, obliged to emote for us to win our sympathy. The accused may be fighting to retain control, or may be drained of emotion after months of awaiting trial. Leave the 5-cent psychiatry to Lucy Van Pelt.

72. *Spiraling cost of living (or inflation)*

A spiral is a curve with an ever-longer radius. It doesn't necessarily go up. The term is embarassingly trite. If you must use comic-book terms like "jump", "zoom" and "plunge" to describe economic events, "soar" is a more appropriate cliche. "Rise" is accurate, and free of hype. "Inflation", of course, implies increase, and so needs no directional modifier.

73. *Spell out*

There are many figures of speech having to do with providing information. "Spell out" is the most threadbare of the lot. "Outline", "provide details of", "describe" are workable.

74. *Split quote*

"The Mayor," said Smith, "may support the proposal." Read that to someone, then ask who said what.

75. *Streamline*

A cliche, when describing organizational or procedural reform. Consider "simplify", "revise", "improve", "abbreviate", etc.

76. *Sustain/suffer*

In describing an injury, "suffer" is preferred. "Sustain" is police jargon.

77. *Synonyms for "say"*

The Voice of America, mindful that many of its listeners are not fluent in English, wants "say, says or said" used in sentences involving quotes. Most everywhere else, synonyms are desirable. But be careful. "State" is stiff, "aver" is outside most people's vocabularies, "claim" implies doubtful veracity, "assert" has an aggressive connotation, "declare" sounds formal ("proclaim" even more so), and "allege" sounds legalistic.

78. *Task force*

Like "blue-ribbon commission", this cliche is mostly the creature of public officials. Let's not help them. "Committee" or "study group" may suffice.

79. *Temblor*

Wire-service and scientific term for an earthquake. (Notice that there is no "r" after the "T".) "Quake", "tremor", "jolt" and "shock" are far more conversational.

80. *Tense calm*

Found in prisons and inner-city neighborhoods, as they exist in newswriters' minds. An oxymoron, intended to indicate an absence of violence. Writers would be more inclined to use "tension", had they not already borrowed that word to euphemize low-level violence.

81. *That/which/who*

If this is your biggest failing, you're in good shape. "That" introduces a defining clause: "This is the house that Jack built." "Which" introduces a parenthetical clause: "The company, which announced a third-quarter loss of a million dollars, declared bankruptcy today." But if you're talking about a person, you would use "who" in either example.

82. *Thief/Robber/Burglar*

All three take things: a thief by stealth or secrecy, a robber by force or fear, and a burglar by breaking and entering of premises. Despite the differentiations among perpetrators, the victim has been robbed, and his belongings have been stolen.

83. *A total of*

Unnecessary, unless preceding copy has cited sub-totals.

84. *Tragedy*

The word alludes to the downfull of a great or mighty figure, at least partly because of an inherent fault (Bernstein). It is not a synonym for misfortune, or even untimely death. There is no handy label for the accidential death of a worthy young mother. As writers of news, we may do best by allowing the facts to speak for themselves—which they do.

85. *Unattributed lead*

"The state's higher education system is in trouble. So says a new report . . ." That may be acceptable in print. But in broadcast writing, the attribution always precedes the quoted material.

86. *Underground tunnel*

What other kind is there?

87. *Unintentional inclusion*

A real reporter on a real network wrote a story about the annual White House Easter egg roll that began: "The biggest collection of clowns in Washington has been assembled here at the White House. They're tall and short, skinny and fat. Some in baggy pants with big red noses. Others on stilts with brightly colored hair. The Vice President is here too . . ." Whether he deserves it or not, Vice President Quayle receives plenty of intentional abuse. This unintended instance should have been spotted before it got on the air.

88. *Unnamed/Unidentified*

That "unnamed source" we hear about every so often certainly has a name. But he has not been identified to reporters.

89. *Verdict/ruling*

Juries return verdicts. Judges issue rulings, opinions or findings.

90. *We/You*

Take care when relating a story to the audience by using the second person. "We'll soon be paying more for gasoline" alienates the person who doesn't own a car. "As you head to the beach this weekend . . ." has no relevance to a shut-in. "The Legislature wants to raise your taxes . . ." comes dangerously close to being a political statement.

91. *Whether or not*

"Whether or not" is acceptable in the sense of "regardless of whether." But when "whether" is used meaning "if", "or not" is unnecessary.

APPENDIX 3

Sample Newscasts

WEEI Local Briefs, 8:58 am, September 1, 1991:

This is U-Haul weekend in Boston's student neighborhoods. An estimated 77-thousand students are arriving at, or returning to college today and tomorrow.	This story as a lead? Keep in mind: 77-thousand people. And, this is a Saturday, with no breaking stories.
The Boston Globe says a survey it commissioned finds 43 percent of respondents willing to move out of the city if they could. Crime and poor economic conditions were the chief reasons given.	"A published report" would be a cop-out. Simple structure: Who-what-why.
At-large city council candidate Frank Costello found racist graffiti on his South Boston home and several cars nearby yesterday. The graffiti attacked Costello and Mayor Flynn as—quote—nigger lovers.	Would have been less cumbersome without "At-large". A general broadcast rule is to let inflection, not the word "quote", set off direct quotes. But given this specific quote, I wanted to distance myself.

High bacteria counts have been recorded in New Bedford's drinking water. As a result, New Bedford residents are asked to boil their water at least until Tuesday.	In New Bedford, this would lead. But my station's signal was weak in that city. This could be structured differently. In New Bedford, the boil-water message would be on top.

WEEI News, 12 noon, September 1, 1991:

MAJOR/SOV—Chris Powell	Slug and identification of sound.
British Prime Minister John Major is in Moscow today, for a nine-hour visit, the first by any western leader since the coup. ABC's Chris Powell has more:	This was the day's breaking story, with frequent updates. The attempted coup against President Gorbachev was less than a month earlier.
CT :37 Std	Abbreviation for "Standard signoff".

SOV/BUSH—Thomas Ginsburg	
President Bush is hinting that the U-S may be ready to give diplomatic recognition to the Baltic republics of Lithuania, Estonia and Latvia. AP Correspondent Thomas Ginsburg says the feeling in Moscow is that it's a given:	Second story stays international. "Hints" may be preferable to "is hinting". If Ginsburg piece had been a voicer or wrap, I would have omitted the label in the intro, because he would have signed off. But here, he was being used as an actuality.
CT :14 ". . . independence."	

LITH/FESTIVAL—Rita Dapkus	
Word of the probable U-S recognition is stirring rejoicing in Vilnius. Rita Dapkus, director of the Lithuanian Information Bureau, says celebration is already underway:	Logical reaction piece to the preceding story.
CT :12 ". . . a festival."	

STUDENT/MOVE

This is the weekend that rental trailer companies love, and neighbors in student sections of town dread. It's when tens of thousands of college students return to campus, accompanied by trailers, vans and station wagons full of belongings. Some arrived a day or two early. But the largest wave arrives today and tomorrow.

Four stories in, we finally go local. Lead sentence is soft, intended mostly to stir listener's curiosity. The real lead, "students return", waits til first development sentence.

Wrapup sentence contains look-ahead element.

M/FENWAY

Boston police are looking for clues in the slaying of a 29-year-old man. Timothy Bailey was found dead early yesterday in his Brookline Avenue apartment. An autopsy revealed he died of asphyxiation and stab wounds. No arrests have been made. Boston homicide detectives are investigating.

Slug "M" for murder.

Second-day lead.
"Murder" is preferable to tabloid "slaying". Who-what-when-where, all in one sentence.

Hmmm . . . this sentence repeats the lead. No excuse, sir.

M/BEVERLY

An emotional funeral service was held yesterday for Amy Carnivale, the 14-year-old Beverly cheerleader murdered two weeks ago. Some 300 relatives and friends filled the church, grieving over the loss. A former boyfriend, 16-year-old Jamie Fuller, is under arrest for the murder, and 19-year-old Michael Maillet has been charged with being an accessory after the fact.

Two "M's" in a row. You see why it gets abbreviated.
Code word for "a lot of people cried."

If she had been a library aide, would it have gotten into the journalese identifier? Guess.

Wrapup sentence should have been broken into two sentences.

CHOOSE / SCHOOL

The Choose-a-School plan takes effect this month, allowing parents to select the schools their children will attend. But the plan will be limited in its scope this fall. Only 17 school districts around the state have agreed to take part. Critics say the plan's funding mechanism is flawed. There's a bill before the Legislature which supporters say would make it more equitable.

Story assumes some listener knowledge of this state program. Story re-written from wire, which re-wrote it from newspaper. Remember, this is a Saturday.

Avoids jargon-y "participate." But includes jargon-y "funding mechanism."

Some don't like sentences that begin with "There is". Here, I defend it as conversational.

SHUTTLE—Ronald Allen

Gone from Logan Airport is the Pan Am Shuttle. Delta bought the Boston-New York-Washington operation from its ailing originator, effective today. Delta Chairman Ronald Allen says his airline will uphold the shuttle's standards:

CT :16
". . . can increase."

A local lead on a piece of national audio service sound. In another newscast, this story may well have been slotted higher up.

WELD / TRADE

Governor Weld, in Asia on a trade mission, has soothed the feelings of an Asian leader who thought he had been snubbed by former Governor Dukakis in 1988. Weld told the president of Keidanren, an influential Japanese business association, that Dukakis did not meet with a delegation because he was out of town on the presidential campaign trail. Weld promised that if the organization sends another delegation to Massachusetts, the visitors will get a warm welcome.

A thinly-rewritten wire story. I put off using it for several hours, but felt it ought to run, so squeezed it in here.

AIDS/BUSH Jon Bascom
Thousands of AIDS activists are heading for Kennebunkport today. ABC's Jon Bascom reports: CT :33 Std

Although placed last in the newscast, this plainly was not a kicker. Kennebunkport is less than 80 miles from Boston, so the story was semi-local.

This newscast runs 4:20, which is longer than the news content of most five-minute newscasts. The explanation is that the preceding program ran short, and that the twelve o'clock news began at 11:58 am. Some of the stories were added at the last minute, when it became apparent that the extra time was available.

APPENDIX 4

Sample Voicers, Wraps, ROSRs

Voicer by ABC News Correspondent Jon Bascom, April 21, 1992

Intro: The Department of Health and Human Services today released their newest data on newborns and their mothers. ABC's Jon Bascom reports: :35

Bascom: The number of low birth weight babies is up while the infant mortality rate is down. The government has new numbers, based on a more expanded birth certificate that went into use three years ago. It shows that too many women are still smoking while pregnant, about one in five. And too many, mostly teenagers, aren't gaining the recommended twenty to twenty-seven pounds in weight. So they give birth to babies that are too small. And while the overall infant mortality rate in the U.S. has shown improvement, this country still ranks 24th in the world in producing healthy babies. Jon Bascom, ABC News, Washington.

Voicer by ABC News Correspondent Ann Compton, April 22, 1992

Intro: President Bush was in Columbus, Ohio, where he delivered the opending remarks at the country's first official celebration of the five hundredth anniversary of Christopher Columbus' discovery of the New World. ABC's Ann Compton reports from Columbus, Ohio: :32

Compton: Air Force One made a low pass over the festival gardens, bringing President Bush to open this five hundred anniversary celebration. Of all the cities in the U.S. named for Christopher Columbus, Ohio's capital is the largest, and it is the site President Bush chose to salute discoveries that have led to what he calls the New World Order. The President then surrendered the microphone to the honorary patron of the festival. Barbara Bush brought and presented an American flag, and she received in return the biggest share of applause. Ann Compton, ABC News, Columbus, Ohio.

Wrap by AP Radio Correspondent Louise Schiavone, April 17, 1992

Intro: Victims of a scam connected to a federal licensing lottery are telling their stories on Capitol Hill. Louise Schiavone reports: :40

Schiavone: James Johnson is a government worker with two small children. A friend of his in Cleveland encouraged him to invest in a communications company offering franchises in wireless cable television. The offer was bogus; Johnson lost about five thousand dollars:

Johnson: It just seemed like such a great opportunity.

Schiavone: Johnson found out too late that the group—Applied Telemedia Engineering and Management—was under federal indictment for unfair and deceptive trade practices. James McIlhenny of the Council of Better Business Bureaus says these scams are enhanced by the fact that these cable licenses are dispensed through a federal lottery. The lesson, he said, is tried but true:

McIlhenny: If it seems too good to be true, it probably is.

Schiavone: This year, cable TV scams are expected to cost the public about 25 million dollars. Louise Schiavone, Capitol Hill.

Wrap by AP Radio Correspondent Louise Schiavone, April 17, 1992

Intro: Some Republicans have a different approach to the House Bank controversy, despite official G-O-P efforts to overthrow a Democratic majority in Congress. Louise Schiavone reports: :39

Schiavone: Minnesota's Vin Weber was a rising star among House Republicans, who rarely missed an opportunity to jab Democrats. You would think he'd like this political commercial:

Commercial: Democrats who can't manage the House Bank are the same Democrats who can't balance the federal budget. And they say it's not their fault. It's time to bounce the Democrats in Congress.

Schiavone: Himself caught in the overdraft net, Weber has decided he doesn't go along with this approach:

Weber: There were no victims in this. Nobody was hurt. Nobody was out any money. That's important.

Schiavone: Weber has decided to retire from Congress after six terms in office. Louise Schiavone, Capitol Hill.

Transcript of ROSR done on March 21, 1981, by Bob Michaels of WPOP (AM), Hartford, at Ku Klux Klan march and counter-demonstration, Meriden, Connecticut.

Sound (under all):	crowd shouting
Michaels:	There's a constant barrage of rocks and bottles, all kinds of flying debris, as the Klan works its way up the street in Meriden. The police are wearing helmets, still trying to dodge all the projectiles that are coming. It's chaotic. Klansmen being hit by rocks, rocks being thrown from all directions. Bottles, too, you can hear them crashing in the background.
Sound:	Breaking bottles
Michaels:	They're picking up now, they're running. The Klansmen are running.
Voice:	You better run! We're gonna kill you . . .
Michaels:	There are bottles . . . cans . . . all kinds of things.
Sound:	Car horn, drawn out.
Michaels:	A cameraman . . . a cameraman was just hit, he just fell on the ground. (panting, as Michaels runs) A police car is running interference for a group of Ku Klux Klansmen, white-sheeted, running down the main street here in Meriden. Rocks and bottles . . .
Sound:	Breaking glass.
Michaels:	. . . have been throwing—that Klansman was just hit on the head with a bottle. (panting) It's a chaotic situation. A police car . . .
Sound:	Voices, nearby, garbled.
Michaels:	. . . running ahead. (panting) Klansmen running, trying to stay low to the ground, protect them-

	selves against projectiles. One Klansman's white robe is all bloodied.
Sound:	Car or motorcycle, accelerating.
Michaels:	A gauntlet of police, running up the street, trying to protect the Klansmen. A rock heaved right near where I'm standing. (panting)
Sound:	Angry shouts.
Michaels:	It's hard to see where the rocks and bottles are coming from, but they're coming from all over. More of them. Klansmen running up the street. You heard the sound of a rock, just now, from behind. Running along myself, trying to escape the projectiles that are being thrown. Nightstick, helmeted policemen, running up the street. Ku Klux Klansmen . . .
Sound:	Emergency vehicle horn. (panting) The Klansmen . . .
Sound:	Young voice, garbled.
Michaels:	(panting) All kinds of rocks.
Sound:	Motorcycles.
Michaels:	Somebody threw a rock at a Klansman. How come?
Voice:	Yes, I did.
Michaels:	How come?
Voice:	Because they have to get out of this town. This town is not for them. They got no rights over here . . .
Michaels:	Don't you think they have a right to protest?
Voice:	No, no way.
Michaels:	Aren't you afraid of arrest?
Voice:	No, I . . . No, nobody's afraid of arrest. They gonna get out of here before they kill 'em.

Michaels:	All kinds of rocks and bottles being thrown. Police cars in Meriden, pulling out now with some Klansmen in them . . .
Sound:	Police siren. Shouts. Breaking bottle.
Michaels:	It's chaos here. Policemen being pelted now, as well. (panting)
Sound:	Crowd shouting, "Get out of here!", etc . . .
Michaels:	One lone Klansman seeking refuge behind a line of policemen.
Sound:	Crowd shouting.
Voice:	Talk about people throwing rocks!
Voice:	You want violence? We give you violence!
Michaels:	One Ku Klux Klansman running as if he doesn't know where to go. He's being escorted by a policeman now. They're rushing after him.
Sound:	More shouting.
Michaels:	All kinds of projectiles. A clock . . .
Sound:	Shouting.
Voice:	The cops and the Klan work hand in hand!
Michaels:	A line of policemen, standing along the street. A crowd taunting them, "The cops and the Klan work hand in hand." Projectiles being thrown into the crowd as well. (panting)
Voice:	What a fucking mess . . .
Michaels:	Police informing people to move on out now . . .

(TAPE ENDS)

NOTE: The transcript is of the unedited tape. Shorter portions were used for broadcast.

(Transcript of live broadcast of demolition of Travelers Building, Boston, MA, March 6, 1988, by Chuck Crouse, WEEI (AM).

Voice on bullhorn:	The one-minute siren!
Crouse:	There you go, you just heard it from the man. The one-minute siren has just been sounded. And all the reporters, and oh my gosh, there must be five or six hundred members of the general public standing here, all standing at the Northern Avenue intersection with Atlantic Avenue. We are facing, across the Central Artery, the Travelers Building, sixteen stories tall now. Controlled Demolition, Incorporated, of Phoenix has placed explosive charges, about three hundred pounds of charges around that building. You wouldn't believe what three hundred pounds can do to a building that's sixteen stories tall. If you've worked in that building and have fond memories of it, say goodbye to it; if you never thought it was much of a building to start with—you didn't like the architectural style, you won't have to worry about it much longer. All that masonry, all that steel, all that glass is about to come down. They're not giving us a second-by-second countdown, so we'll just hear a huge boom when it happens . . . actually, a series of booms. I've been told it sounds like fireworks.
Voice:	Fifteen seconds!
Crouse:	Fifteen seconds, we've just been told. All right. We can count it down, we can just kind of wait here. I've been told the side of the building that is closest to us will go down first.
Voice:	Six, five, (crowd joins in) four, three . . .
Crouse:	There you go, that's the countdown, and uh, let's . . .
Sound:	Series of loud detonations

Crouse: An amazing thing to watch! Just absolutely amazing! A sixteen-story building breaks into little pieces and collapses. A huge cloud, a billowing cloud of grey dirt and dust and who knows whatever else, is crossing the Central Artery and coming our way. And we're all hoping that nothing too big is in that cloud. We've been told to expect to get pretty filthy. The entire building went down in perhaps ten seconds, in a succession of loud percussions. And all the crowd here, you can hear them just cheering and expressing amazement at the whole thing. The cloud of dirt and dust is perhaps a hundred feet away from us now, and we're gonna see how much a couple of sheets of paper can do, to keep the stuff off of me here. The people have got handkerchiefs over their faces, and now they're pushing through the press area, trying to get out. They'd been told they shouldn't be at this location because there'd be all the debris. And they didn't believe the man with the bullhorn, and now they're trying to crowd through. So far, we're not seeing anything fairly large. As a matter of fact, there's nothing but this huge cloud, so we can't tell you how big the pile of rubble is. We were told it would be about thirty feet high. Then this will all be cleared away. Around the area of the Travelers Building, earth was put down, so that heavier items falling on the ground would not create too much damage in the pavement. One of the things that was a concern to the demolition company was a huge air conditioning unit that was sitting up on the roof of the building. Big thing, rather heavy. They were hoping it would go straight down, but they couldn't be absolutely sure. Well, one of the things that was happening right during the explosion, the air conditioning unit let go on the, oh, what would be about the west end, and fell what appeared to be straight down. So that huge air conditioning unit should be right down in the middle of the rubble, exactly where they want it to be. All right, now the debris is starting to fall out of the air, and it seems to be all little bits of ash and dust and so on . . . nothing big. And people are covering their faces with their hands and Kleenex and so on. So the Travelers Building is gone, and the sunshine of a Boston morning is becoming kind of clouded right now. But you'll be seeing it on television tonight. You'll probably see the building go down six or seven times, and no doubt somebody will get the bright idea to play the tape backwards, so they can watch it go back up again. It will not go back up. In its place will go up a four hundred million dollar project of several buildings called 125 High Street, being built by a local Boston development company. So it's been an exciting morning . . . No, now the cloud is clearing up, and you can see International Place looming through the cloud, and you cannot see the Traveler's building. Just an amazing thing to see happening. Reporting live from Atlantic Avenue and Northern Avenue, I'm Chuck Crouse, WEEI 590 News.

APPENDIX 5

Rewriting a News Release

The following page is an actual release. The student may wish to try rewriting it before turning to several sample rewrites prepared by the author:

Release rewritten as a headline:

The Revenue Department will close seven offices.	Mostly a tease. Leaves several major questions unanswered.

Release rewritten as one-sentence brief:

The State Revenue Department, facing a nine-million dollar budget cut, says it'll close seven of its ten district offices.	Covers the basics, including "seven of ten" and tells why, but omits when and where. Could add ". . . in July", if not worried by overly-long sentence.

DOR NewsRelease

Commonwealth of Massachusetts **Department of Revenue**

For Release: April 17, 1992

Contact: Michelle Andrews

DEPARTMENT OF REVENUE TO CLOSE 7 OF 10 DISTRICT TAX OFFICES; WORCESTER, SPRINGFIELD AND FALL RIVER OFFICES TO REMAIN OPEN

As part of a plan to absorb a proposed $8.9 million cut in its FY93 tax administration operating budget, the Department of Revenue will close seven of its 10 district offices at the end of the fiscal year, Revenue Commissioner Mitchell Adams announced today. District offices in Worcester, Springfield and Fall River as well as the Boston taxpayer assistance headquarters will remain open, but tax offices in Brockton, Fitchburg, Greenfield, Hyannis, Lowell, Pittsfield and Wakefield will close. By closing the offices, DOR will save more than three quarters of a million dollars in rent and operating costs next fiscal year.

"There are no easy answers or painless choices here," said Adams. "In order to meet our budget target for fiscal '93, we have no choice but to close district offices by the end of this fiscal year," said Adams. "Fortunately, many of the taxpayer inquiries we have traditionally handled at the district office level can be answered by telephone through our statewide toll-free taxpayer assistance number. We are also looking at a number of options, including hiring seasonal staff, that would allow us to maintain a regional taxpayer assistance presence during the busy filing season."

Last year, approximately 190,000 taxpayers visited DOR's 10 district offices for tax assistance. In addition to taxpayer assistance staff, district offices are staffed by audit, collections and criminal investigations personnel.

Although they will no longer offer taxpayer assistance, the facilities in Brockton, Lowell and Pittsfield will not actually close their doors. DOR plans to move staff from its Child Support Enforcement (CSE) Division into the space vacated by the tax administration operations in these towns. The move will allow DOR to consolidate CSE staff on the north and south shores into regional offices as well as relocate staff in Pittsfield into better office space with improved computer capability.

The proposed budget cut will also require layoffs of approximately 215 DOR staff later this spring. Although the final layoff plan has not been finalized, layoffs will occur by job function rather than geographic location. This means that some of the staff in the district offices slated to close will be reassigned to other offices, while others will be laid off.

Release rewritten as two-sentence reader:

The state Revenue Department say's it'll close seven of its ten district tax offices. The cuts are to take effect in July, because of a nine-million dollar cut in the Governor's proposed budget.	Gets in the when and expands on the why, but still omits which offices will be closed. This version notes that cuts are only "proposed", not actually enacted.

Release rewritten as three-sentence reader:

The state Revenue Department says seven of its ten district tax offices will close in July, if a nine-million dollar cut in the Governor's proposed budget goes through. Offices targeted are in Brockton, Fitchburg, Greenfield, Hyannis, Lowell, Pittsfield and Wakefield. Revenue Commissioner Mitchell Adams says 215 staffers will be let go as well.	In this version, sentences are longer. In practice, you'd probably only list the office(s) in or closest to your community. In this version, we name the agency head and include layoffs.

Release rewritten as reporter voicer:

Intro: Seven state tax offices are on the chopping block. Jo Doakes reports:

Reporter: Revenue Commissioner Mitchell Adams says he has a way to live with the nine-million dollar cut his agency will take in the Governor's proposed budget. He's ready to close seven of the ten district tax offices and lay off 215 Revenue Department staffers. The offices are in Brockton, Fitchburg, Greenfield, Hyannis, Lowell, Pittsfield and Wakefield. Offices in Worcester, Springfield and Fall River would stay open, along with Boston headquarters. The closings aren't a done deal; the Legislature has

> yet to debate the budget, and could vote to give the department enough money to keep those offices open. Jo Doakes, WXXX News.

(Note that the last sentence is not based on facts contained in the news release. But reporters are expected to know the process and be able to tell how it relates to developments.)

APPENDIX 6

Ten How-To's They Didn't Teach in College

1. *How to estimate a crowd:* Try to stand off to the side of the crowd, with an overall view. Select an area of limited size, and count the number of people in that area. Then mentally superimpose that area over the rest of the crowd, section by section. Multiply the number of people in the "test" area by the number of times that area can be fit over the total crowd. Fudge the result upward or downward if the crowd density varies in one place or another. Members of the public—and police—often overestimate crowd sizes.

2. *How to solder:* Gather a low-wattage soldering pencil (25 watts is common), a roll of rosin-core solder, a small file, a pen knife and a pair of needle-nose pliers. Plug in the soldering pencil and give it at least five minutes to warm up. Rest the tip on the formed-wire rest that came with the tool, or on some heatproof substance. Using the pen knife, strip no more than half an inch of insulation from the wires to be soldered. Using the needle-nose pliers, bend the end of each wire into a J-shaped hook. Hook together the two ends to be soldered and crimp together with pliers. (Alternate method: twist the ends of

the wires together.) Touch the tip of the soldering pencil to the joint, and leave it there for about ten seconds—long enough to heat up the wires. Then touch the solder to the wire joint (not to the iron).

After a few seconds, the solder will flow over the joint. The joint should be held immobile as you remove the tip of the soldering pencil, allowing the solder to cool. A good joint has enough solder on it to hold the wires together, but does not have a gob of excess solder. The solder should look shiny, not grainy. Feel free to unsolder the joint and try again. If the tip of the pencil becomes covered with scale and crud, impeding efficient heat transfer, use the file to clean the tip.

3. *How to identify multiple speakers* (as at a panel discussion or joint news conference) *on your tape:* Run an extension mic cord from your mic on the lectern to the recorder which rests in your lap. As each speaker begins or ends his or her remarks, briefly pull the mic plug from your recorder's mic jack, thereby activating the built-in mic. Bend down and speak the person's name into the built-in mic. Then re-insert the mic plug in its jack.

4. *How to get through a dense crowd:* Hold a "badge of authority" in front of you—a microphone, walkie-talkie or hand-held cellular phone—while repeating, "Coming through, please; coming through, please . . ."

5. *How to get out of an employment contract when the boss won't let you go:* Wait a couple of days, then provoke an argument, during the course of which you insult your boss' religion. There are risks, but you *will* be fired.

6. *How to start a conversation with the famous journalist who you discover is standing or sitting right next to you:* Do not introduce yourself, unless there's some good reason why he or she would recognize your name. Offhand small talk, as if you *always* sit next to David Broder, is less threatening than "Oh, I've always admired your work", which creates a stratified relationship.

7. *How to win over the harried official who's already talked to twenty reporters in the hour since the building collapsed:* Combine a recognition of his human problem with a non-threatening request: "I'll bet you're about thirty seconds away from laryngitis. My question will take twenty-nine seconds to answer."

8. *How to keep your equipment from being stolen from your car or hotel room* (short of carrying it with you): Follow the adage "hide in plain sight". Keep it in a crumpled brown paper bag, or in a corrugated cardboard box neatly labelled "Textbooks". Expensive aluminum carrying cases shout out that there's something valuable inside.

9. *How to establish a fact that is not being officially released* (e. g., Was someone killed in the accident?): Ask questions that assume the fact being sought (Do you have an ID yet on the person killed in that crash?). Three answers are possible. 1. "Not yet." (Or, "Yes, John Doe, of . . ."), which confirms the death. 2. "No one was killed in that accident.", which tells you your information was wrong. 3. "What makes you think anyone was killed? We're not releasing any details yet.", which means, "Nice try, but it didn't work."

10. *How to be prepared if the axe should fall suddenly:* Make sure your home stereo system includes a dual (dubbing) cassette deck; frequently update your home tape archives; frequently update your home file of story and newscast scripts; and keep at home a list of stations you'd want to apply to.

APPENDIX 7

Journalists' Organizations

Alpha Epsilon Rho (AERho)
College of Journalism
University of South Carolina
Columbia, SC 29208

303/777-3324
John Lopiccolo, national executive secretary

Asian American Journalists Association (AAJA)
1765 Sutter Street
Room 1000
San Francisco, CA 94115

415/346-2051
Valerie Chow Bush, executive director

Association for Education in Journalism and Mass Communications (AEJMC)
University of South Carolina
1621 College Street
Columbia, SC 29208-0251

803/777-2005
Jennifer McGill, executive director

Associated Press Broadcasters, Inc. (APB)
1825 K Street, NW
Suite 615
Washington, DC 20006

202/955-7236
Ruth Domboski, executive director

International Radio & Television Society (IRTS)
599 Lexington Avenue
New York, NY 10170

212/867-6650
Stephen B. Labunski, executive director

National Association of Black Journalists (NABJ)
11600 Sunrise Valley Drive
Reston, VA 22091

703/648-1270
Sidmel Estes-Sumpter, executive director

National Association of Broadcasters (NAB)
1771 N Street, NW
Washington, DC 20036

202/429-5300
Edward O. Fritts, president

National Association of Hispanic Journalists (NAHJ)
529 14th Street, NW
Suite 1193
Washington, DC 20045

202/662-7145
Jose D. McMurray, executive director

Radio-Television News Directors Association (RTNDA)
1000 Connecticut Avenue, NW

Suite 615
Washington, DC 20036

202/659-6510
David Bartlett, president

Society of Professional Journalists (SPJ)
P.O. Box 77
16 S. Jackson
Greencastle, IN 46135

317/653-3333
Ernie Ford, executive director

APPENDIX 8

Glossary

Actuality: An edited excerpt of recorded sound, usually a newsmaker's voice, but also natural news-related sound. Also Sound bite, Cut (q.v.), Wild sound (q.v.)

Air cue: On-air program, heard via radio, telephone or line, which lets a reporter know when to begin a live report.

AGC: Automatic Gain Control. Electronic circuitry in a recorder or other equipment, which maintains sound volume within acceptable limits without requiring manual adjustment.

AGC-defeat switch: A switch (sometimes labelled "Music") which bypasses AGC circuitry, permitting manual volume control.

Alligator clips: Spring-loaded metal clips, especially when attached to one end of a patch cord.

Ambient noise: The natural sounds heard in a given area, which may enhance or detract from a field report. Can be controlled by proper mic placement.

Anchor intro: Anchor's copy introducing a live or recorded report. (See also Hard lead.)

Antenna: A metallic device for transmitting or receiving radio signals. At an AM station, it's the entire tower. At an FM station, it's one or more "bays" at or near the top of the tower. On portable gear, the direction in which the antenna is pointed may affect performance.

Broadcast loop: A telephone circuit, electronically equalized for high audio quality. Also called Broadcast Line.

Cans: Headphones. A set with different sound in each earphone, as in a control room, is called Split Cans.

Cardioid microphone: A microphone with directional pickup pattern, strongest to the front, weakest to the rear.

Codec: Coder-Decoder. Required at each end of a digital telephone line. Functionally similar to computer modem.

Cut: (n.): On tape, an actuality; on audio news service, any edited piece of sound. (v.): To edit tape, though process may involve dubbing more often than physical cutting of tape.

DAT: Digital Audio Tape. Magnetic tape technology using tape cassettes different from conventional analog tape cassettes.

Daisy chain: Use of one or more patch cords (see Dub cord) to allow more than one recorder to record from a single mic or other audio source. The cord goes from the earphone jack of recorder A to the mic jack of recorder B.

Development sentence: Sentence(s) following the Lead sentence (q.v.), advancing the narrative of a news story.

Dial-up telephone: The usual kind, available virtually everywhere, but offering limited audio quality. Applies equally to touch-tone or rotary-dial models.

Dial pad: The twelve buttons found on a touch-tone telephone, also on some telephone interface equipment.

Digital telephony: Telephone technology achieving high audio quality by converting analog sound to digital signals for transmission. Common modes are ISDN and Switched 56.

Dub: To record all or part of a recording on another recording device. Media may be similar or different.

Dub cord: A patch cord with attenuating resistors built into it, used for dubbing between cassette recorders.

Fatal: Oral shorthand for fatal traffic accident. Seldom used on air. Also Double fatal, Pedestrian fatal, etc.

Fiber-optics: Technology using tiny strands of flexible glass in place of wires to transmit signals.

Fishpole: A hand-held microphone boom, often telescoping.

Frequency response: Audio performance of a given piece of equipment, expressed in Herz (cycles per second). A unit that is "flat" (consistent) from 50 to 15,000 Hz is said to have excellent frequency response.

Gang-bang: A group interview, usually unplanned, with several reporters jointly questioning a single newsmaker.

Handoff: The conclusion of reporter piece, introducing another reporter directly, without involvement of anchor.

Hard lead: An anchor intro to reporter piece, in which the anchor gives the core facts of story.

Heads: A series of short news stories, usually one sentence each. Also Briefs.

Hybrid: An electronic interface to a telephone system, usually in-studio, providing improved quality for taped interviews or live conversations.

Integral newscast: A newscast written on a single sheet of paper (or more, as length dictates), not made up of a stack of separate news stories.

ISDN: Integrated Services Digital Network. See Digital telephony.

Kicker: A short news story, usually humorous, often used to conclude a newscast.

Lead sentence: The first sentence in a news story, setting forth the basic facts and drawing the listener's attention.

Line level: An audio signal which has been amplified, loud enough to drive an earphone, but too loud to be fed into a mic-level (q.v.) input. Doing so produces a distorted, unusable recording.

Mic level: Weak audio signal, such as comes from a microphone, tape head, turntable cartridge. Requires amplification. Mic-level inputs lead to preamplifier circuits.

Mini-plug/jack: 1/8″ diameter connectors, common on most cassette recorders and some other consumer electronics equipment.

Modem: Modulator-Demodulator. Converts computer data into a modulated analog signal for transmission on a conventional telephone line.

MOS: Man On the Street. Interview(s) done with members of the public, usually outdoors, to get a sampling of public opinion or reaction to an event.

Mult box: Multiple-outlet feed box, provided by organizers of some events, to allow recording equipment to be plugged in. Obviates need for cluster of mics in front of speaker(s). Mic-level sound through XLR outlets is most common.

Next-day lead: A revised version of a news story whose lead makes it suitable for use the next day.

Noise-cancelling microphone: Highly directional microphone intended for use in very noisy locations.

Off-axis: Away from the axis, typically of a microphone. If a mic is pointed straight ahead, its axis is toward 12 o'clock. Sound coming from 3 o'clock, for example, would 90 degrees off-axis.

Omnidirectional microphone: A microphone which is equally sensitive to sounds coming from all directions.

One-on-One: An interview involving one reporter and one newsmaker.

Overmodulation: The electrical effect of sounds too loud for circuitry to handle. The result is audible distortion.

P.A.: At news events, the public address system. In public agencies, Public Affairs (public relations); in your station's transmitter, the power amplifier.

Podium sound: what is usually obtained from a mult box: sound from the mic in the front of the room. The structure supporting the mic, the speaker's copy, a reading light, etc, is actually a lectern, but people often call it a podium.

Proximity effect: A buildup in low-frequency response by many mics when the speaker is closer than three inches (approx.)

Q&A: An actuality in which the reporter is heard asking a question of the newsmaker. Also, an actuality in which the reporter him/herself is responding to a question.

RENG: Radio Electronic News-Gathering. Usually applied to use of cellular phones, RPU (q.v.) and two-way radio (q.v) in reporting news, often live.

ROSR: Radio On-Scene Report. A recorded report, usually adlibbed, in which the reporter describes events as they happen.

RPU: Remote Pick-Up. Compact transmitters, often with receivers built in, operating on specified frequencies, providing high-quality audio from a remote location.

Raw tape: Unedited tape, usually in the context of turning it over to someone else to edit.

Reader: A news story read by the anchor within a newscast. As distinct from voicers, wraps, ROSR's, which are voiced by people other than the anchor.

Remote: A broadcast, usually scheduled, originating away from the station. Applies to entertainment or public affairs programming more often than to news reporting.

Remote mixer: A mixer/amplifier suitable for use in remote broadcasts. Also used for small-scale production chores.

Reverse cue: A transmission over a walkie-talkie to a reporter waiting to begin a live report, who is otherwise unable to hear the station for a cue.

Second-line lead: A reporter piece written so that the anchor intro contains the core of the story (see Hard lead), allowing the reporter to concentrate on additional details.

Self-contained: A reporter piece in which the reporter introduces him/herself, requiring no anchor intro.

Shotgun microphone: A highly directional mic, suitable for picking up sound from a distance.

Sidebar: Newspaper term for a story containing some peripheral aspect of a major story, printed adjacent to the major story. In broadcasting, the term suggests that the aspect covered by the reporter is not a major one.

Sidekick: A broadcaster who regularly appears on a disc jockey or talk show in a secondary capacity. May sometimes read news, but is usually not presented as a serious news person.

Sign-off: The conclusion of a reporter piece, usually containing the reporter's name and location and the station's call letters and slogan. Also Lockout.

Stringer: A news person who files occasional pieces with a station from a distant location, usually paid by the piece.

Stump speech: A candidate's usual speech, seldom varying except to acknowledge the city being visited or the group being addressed.

Two-way radio: Transmitter-receiver equipment licensed to certain business frequencies, free of interference from other users but offering limited audio quality.

Voicer: A reporter piece, usually recorded, containing no actuality.

Voicer, on-scene: A voicer recorded at a location chosen for identifiable background sounds.

Wild sound: Recorded non-verbal material such as music, crowd noise, or other sounds which help to tell a story.

Wire capture: A feature of newsroom computer systems, in which wire service material bypasses the printer and is saved on hard disk for editing at the newsperson's convenience.

Work tape: A tape onto which material is recorded for editing convenience. Used in producing wraps and other packages which go on the air.

Wrap: A reporter piece which incorporates one or more actualities.

Wrapup sentence: The final sentence in a news story, containing facts deemed worthy of inclusion but not accommodated earlier in the story. Often has a look-ahead element.

XLR: Generic term for common professional audio connectors, 5/8″ in diameter and having three pins. Sometimes called Cannon plugs, after the company originating the design.

Zoo: Generic term for morning programs on music stations which feature several personalities, listener interaction and humor often billed as zany, irreverent or outrageous.

Index

About the Author

Chuck Crouse began his broadcasting career in 1957, as a studio engineer at WERE AM/FM, Cleveland. He moved into radio news in 1959, at WOSU AM/FM, Columbus, Ohio. Since then, he has reported radio news in Norwalk, Ohio; Cleveland; Fort Wayne; Hartford; New Haven; New York City and Boston. From 1974 until 1991, he reported and anchored at all-news WEEI (AM), Boston. He is now a freelance reporter for ABC News. Since 1985, Crouse has written the column "Reporting for Radio" and occasional feature articles for the RTNDA *Communicator.* Crouse's major avocation is railroading, and he is the author of the 1990 book, "Budd Car: The RDC Story." He lives with his wife, Ginny, in Dedham, Massachusetts. Their daughter, Angie, attends Arizona State University.

Books and Audio Cassettes for Broadcasters

How to Read Copy

Professionals' Guide to Delivering Voice-Overs and Broadcast Commercials
Adrian Cronauer

A book for both professional announcers and aspiring broadcasters. The goal is straightforward: To help announcers sound natural on the air (a 25-minute audio cassette produced by Cronauer included FREE with the book).

ISBN 0-929387-14-7, clothbound, 200 pp., $29.95

Broadcast Voice Handbook

How to Polish Your On-Air Delivery
(co-published with the RTNDA)
Ann S. Utterback, Ph.D.

The book begins with the production of the breath and moves through producing and resonating sound waves, to the articulation of sound, and, finally, the methods of stressing meaning.

ISBN 0-929387-16-3, clothbound, 264 pp., $26.95

Audio Cassettes
Vocal Expressiveness

Dr. Ann S. Utterback explains two methods to use to bring news stories to life: script making and an interpersonal communication approach.

Vocal Exercises

Dr. Utterback leads you step-by-step through exercises and drills to improve breathing, increase resonance, and polish articulation.

Coping with Stress

Dr. Utterback talks about stress—what it is, how it affects the body and the voice, and ways to begin to stress-proof your life. Side two offers a series of relaxation techniques including a guided relaxation period.

All audiocassettes co-produced with the RTNDA, $19.95

Writing Broadcast News
Shorter, Sharper, Stronger
Mervin Block

Hundreds of examples from local and network news, radio and TV—with rewrites and commentary.

ISBN 0-933893-20-5, clothbound, 231 pp., $24.95

Rewriting Network News
WorthWatching Tips from 345 TV and Radio Scripts
Mervin Block

Rewriting Network News showcases mistakes, network mistakes. These examples, plus corrections and revisions, show how to write more effective broadcast copy.

ISBN 0-929387-15-5, clothbound, 220 pp., $24.95

Breaking into Broadcasting

Getting a Good Job that Leads to the Top
Donn Pearlman

Advice on how to find, keep and use that first job in television or radio.

ISBN 0-933893-16-7, clothbound, 224 pp., $15.95

Broadcasting Books, c/o RTNDA, 1000 Connecticut Ave., Suite 615, Washington, DC 20006. (202) 659-6510. Bonus Books, 160 E. Illinois Street, Chicago, IL 60611. (312) 467-0580